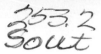

comprehensive pastoral care

ENABLING
THE LAITY
TO SHARE IN
PASTORAL
MINISTRY

Samuel Southard

JUDSON PRESS
Valley Forge

COMPREHENSIVE PASTORAL CARE

Library of Congress Cataloging in Publication Data

Southard, Samuel.
  Comprehensive pastoral care.

  Includes bibliographical references.
  1. Pastoral theology. 2. Laity. 3. Church management.
4. Christian leadership. I. Title.
BV4011.S59   253'.2   74-22518
ISBN 0-8170-0655-9

Printed in the U.S.A.

Contents

CHAPTER ONE

Coaching Those Who Care

On our way to a pastors' conference, the minister of a county-seat church turned to the senior minister of a large metropolitan congregation and said, "Don, I've just been elected vice-president of the state convention, and I don't see how I can keep up my pastoral work. It's heavy anyway. What's your solution? Do you still visit—and see people? How do you keep up with the demands? It seems too much to me."

"You really want to know what my plans are?" replied the senior minister. "I plan to get a doctor's degree in counseling and get out of the church about the time I get established in counseling—I'll be fifty-five then. That's my way of solving an insolvable problem."

The insolvable problem is to care for people and still maintain an organization. It is insolvable if shepherding and administering are seen as competing demands upon the pastor's time. But suppose administration was an essential part of the care of individuals. We could then organize for the delivery of more specific service to people when they need us most. This is the solution found by other helping professions which recognize that no professional staff of a church, a clinic, or a hospital can give all that is needed in prevention, crisis intervention, healing, support, direction, and rehabilitation. The new solution is to provide breadth and depth of care through the involvement of a wide range of caring persons in gradations of tasks for which they are trained and motivated.

A New Priority for Pastors

The priorities of a pastor's services are reversed in this system. Instead of going first to the sick and the lonely, the pastor will spend most of the time and attention with the healthy members who then become ministers to the sick and the lonely. Now this does not mean that the pastor does nothing but care for a cadre of helpers. He or she goes with them as a teacher and model of ministry. But the pastor does not go and go and go. There are varieties of service and there are many people who can serve—if they are cared for.

To provide the range of care that is needed today, the professionally trained person must share his or her skills and attitudes more through consultation and education than through direct service. The pastor, doctor, and social worker still serve people, but they begin with the care of those who serve with them. Many persons can do most of what we pastors can do; our special task as pastors is to prepare others for service and support them both through administration and example in that service.

In this book we will see how churches and other agencies have worked together to provide systematic service. Although some of the references will be to theory and plans, most of the chapters are based on actual examples. We will examine the successes and failures of building and maintaining a program in which the clergyperson is coach for those who care.

This sharing of pastoral responsibility begins when you admit that the demands made upon you are unrealistic. You cannot do and be all the things that are expected by experts in counseling, professors of pastoral theology, concerned lay people, exuberant ecclesiastics, or troubled people. Instead of adding more "oughts" to your office, I propose a reduction of obligations to the congregation and a restriction on professional expectations. I am suggesting ways for a minister to do more with what he or she already has—in personal resources, the congregation, and the community. This calls for some relatively simple management skills and a certain amount of humility in the acceptance of the clergyperson's own human limitations. My scheme also requires a joy in serving people as a representative of eternal values and a belief in God that provides the deepest meaning of life.

People in the helping professions are learning how to organize their services to make use of more community resources—family, volunteers, "indigenous" workers—and to decrease the demands for professional assistance. They are beginning to share responsibility with each other as professionals and to trust the "indigenous" worker who does not have their training but who knows the people and the neighborhood.

Most of all, the healing professions are assisting troubled people toward interdependence rather than dependence. We are finding ways to increase self-reliance and self-respect by placing more responsibility upon the individual client and creating a support system in the community upon which the person may call on occasion when the demands or emergencies of life become too great.

The functions of local clergy are magnified in this reality-orientation to service. You are in the community where the people can best be served, rather than in a specialized institution where people are isolated from their normal conduct. You contact people before they are so crisis-ridden that all their self-respect and psychological resources are depleted. Because you serve the healthy and the sick, you can call on one group to serve the other. And, above all else, you lead people toward a transcendent purpose for getting up in the morning, forgiving enemies, living cheerfully with limitations.

What Are My Priorities?

How can you be more of what you want to be as a pastor? From a variety of ministerial surveys we can formulate these basic concerns:

1. "I want to know what my people really need, what really troubles them. What are their strengths and weaknesses?" This concern calls for some system of visitation—or a survey—in the congregation and tactics for knowing and securing assistance from community agencies. The technical management term for this function is "entering the system."

When we have met this need, we will have done what God requires of an adequate shepherd of Israel: "I will seek the lost, and I will bring back the strayed, and I will bind up the crippled, and I will strengthen the weak, and the fat and the strong I will watch over; I will feed them in justice" (Ezekiel 34:16).

To "feed in justice" requires a distribution of time and attention to the healthy, the worried healthy, the early sick, the intermittently ill, and the chronic sufferers. Chapter 2 will present ways in which the various needs can be classified for the sake of developing a program of comprehensive pastoral care.

2. "Will the congregation support this kind of decisive ministry?" The same question is raised in every profession that moves beyond one-to-one direct service to clients who flood into an office. For the minister, and others, there must be some clarification of tasks in this congregation. What is most important? How is this to be reported? Are limitations on the pastor's time, training, and patience recognized and accepted? How will the leadership interpret these limitations to the congregation, and how will the church provide services beyond those which one minister can perform?

Chapter 3 will present the key elements in several successful lay leadership programs of pastoral care. The churches in the survey ranged from large downtown congregations to churches in small towns. The theological style varied from evangelistic witnessing to sophisticated emphasis upon "human potential."

3. "How do I plan for and develop a comprehensive care program in my church?" Seven steps in "participant management" are recommended in chapter 4. These are the same stages through which we move in assisting a troubled individual. The process of church management is a model for

the development of a plan for pastoral care.

4. "I want my church to have an impact in the community." The most difficult problem of United Presbyterian clergymen, reported in a 1969 survey, was "shaping the role of my local church in the community."[1] Some of this need may have been prompted by the "church in the world" emphasis of the sixties. The challenge of the Missionary Structures of the Congregation studies by national and world councils of churches was to rethink the organization and assumptions of a congregation. Was the local church really organized to make an impact in the community?

Most of the answers sought in the sixties were in social action. Why not consider also some changes in pastoral care in order to broaden the area of responsibility and the resources for personal help in the spirit of Christ? To do so requires a view of the church as one of the social systems of a community. The religious community provides goals and motivation to serve governmental, educational, economic, cultural, health and welfare systems. In biblical terms, the church becomes the leaven in the loaf. As the church is thus in the world, it will move toward the goal that Jesus portrayed in numerous

---

[1]*Blue Book,* Part III, 181st General Assembly of the United Presbyterian Church in the United States of America (New York, 1969), p. 29.

parables about the kingdom. (See Matthew 13.)

In chapter 5 we will identify these systems by which people are influenced and examine ways by which the pastor and others involved in a program of pastoral care can enter these systems. As clergy and congregations enter into these systems, they need to examine their motivation. Are they trying to recruit members for the church or to serve people without seeking credit or control? If pastors and lay people apply the saying of Jesus, "For whoever would save his life will lose it, and whoever loses his life for my sake will find it" (Matthew 16:25), they will find new life—and so will others.

Chapter 5 will also present the spirit and content of a training program for church leaders. The emphasis will be upon the contribution that each person can make to the training sessions, and on the way in which the social systems of family and community can aid a person through periods of difficulty. The goal is a combination of individual responsibility and social interdependence.

The apostle Paul wrote of the need both to share or identify with the needs of others and to see that each one is realistic in personal responsibility:

Brethren, if a man is overtaken in any trespass, you who are spiritual should restore him in a spirit of gentleness. Look to yourself, lest you too be tempted. Bear one another's burdens, and so fulfil the law of Christ. For if any one thinks he is something, when he is nothing, he deceives himself. But let each one test his own work, and then his reason to boast will be in himself alone and not in his neighbor. For each man will have to bear his own load (Galatians 6:1-5).

5. "I can't carry all this responsibility alone—*I* need someone to lean on." Where is this support to be found? When Edgar (Ted) Mills and John Koval surveyed stress through questionnaire responses from fifteen thousand Protestant clergy, they found ministers relying upon self-help, prayer, Bible study and meditation, and upon informal conversations with denominational associates or with the wife at home. Although the support from fellow clergy was significant in the study, there was an absence of consultation with "other professionals" about problems in the parish, overwork, and frustration with lack of accomplishment. It seems that the clergy are neglecting opportunities to seek help with pastoral problems from specialists in the helping disciplines. I realize that the opportunities may be limited in some communities, but there are now enough mental health centers throughout the country to duplicate the success of North Carolina and other states in providing training-and-support seminars for clergy with psychiatrists, social workers, psychiatric nurses, clinical psychologists, occupational therapists, and rehabilitation

counselors. Some of the examples from various parts of the U.S. will be examined in chapter 6.

The study by Mills shows a heavy reliance of pastors upon their wives for support in job adjustment problems, overwork, frustration, a death in the family, and personal health problems.[2] This dependence is too much, if it goes beyond seeking general, subjective support of one you love to expecting a detailed analysis of strategy, depth of feeling, and resolution of parishioners' problems. We must separate emotional support from consultation, giving a spouse's love and concern great significance and yet not requiring her or him to evaluate and advise as a role model or professional expert. The latter requirements should be met through formal and informal meetings with other pastors, denominational officials, and community representatives of other helping professions.

Another source of support can come from concerned and competent members of the congregation. Mills and Koval found that ministers do involve congregational leaders in discussions on "personal problems with congregation." This may be read as the minister's own difficulty with individuals or groups. I hope it could become of

[2] The findings on stress resolution and the support system are in chapter 4 of Edgar W. Mills and John P. Koval, *Stress in the Ministry* (Washington, D.C.: Ministry Studies Board, 1971).

some assistance to the minister in dealing with the problems that individuals have with people other than their pastor. We will look at some of the attempts that have been made to use this resource both for the pastor's own difficulties and those of his people.

What Can I Realistically Expect?

One of the problems with texts in any helping profession is that they have, like the lawyers of Jesus' time on earth, created heavy burdens for us to bear. Authors become so enthusiastic about a new plan or procedure that everyone is expected to become an expert in this and related disciplines. Who can bear the weight of all these ideals?

I would aim for more integration of care and counseling into the specific purpose of the ministry, which is to take intelligent action by authority of Christ and his church that will link God's love with human frailty. I would not suggest that every pastor should become the equal of a psychiatrist as a diagnostician, the social worker as a case-finder and manager, or the rehabilitation counselor, marriage and family counselor, or visiting nurse in their competencies.

My desire is that we learn to cooperate with related disciplines, to use their significant contribution to the care of people, and to make our own as representatives of Christ and the church. It is neither just to the individual pastor nor realistic in the light of new growth in related professions for a local clergyperson to think that he or she can do half the work of a dozen professions. That is six times more work than any one person should attempt, and it probably will decrease one's satisfaction in the job to which one has been divinely called and for which one has had some training.

I do not wish to minimize the importance of specialized counseling skills for a few clergypersons who serve as teachers of pastors or as counselors of clergy, and I recognize the necessity of some unique preparation for chaplains in hospitals, industry, and community agencies. But I would not extend the requirements of their training or the assumptions of their practice to local clergy. Instead, I would challenge the trained pastoral counselor to conduct more training and consultation for colleagues in a congregation. As Richard Robertson estimated from his training of over five hundred community clergy in the Bradley Center, Columbus, Georgia, one trainer could work with two hundred parish pastors in a year. One thousand specialist-counselors would thus be needed for the approximately two hundred thousand active parish ministers in the United States.[3]

With more than a thousand ministers already

trained through at least one year of clinical pastoral education, the problem is not to create more specialists but to find ways of training the great majority of pastors in techniques and theories of care and counseling that are appropriate for the limited amount of time that they have available for that service. In this text we are suggesting one direction for such training, which is to develop a system of shared responsibility, pastor-church-community. This is similar to the emphasis of physical and mental health programs upon training and utilization of indigenous workers, professionals, allied health aides, and volunteers. These persons are not only being encouraged to take major responsibility for front-line service; they are also altering the assumption that only a professional with specialized training can really help people in trouble.

What may we expect of ourselves as pastors who realize that we have little time or training for intensive counseling, and who wish to maximize the breadth and depth of pastoral care in church and community? In answering this question, we assume that "pastoral care" is sustaining and guiding

[3]Richard N. Robertson, Leonard T. Maholick, and David S. Shapiro, "The Parish Minister as Counselor: A Dilemma and Challenge," *Pastoral Psychology*, vol. 20, no. 195 (June, 1969), pp. 24-30.

individuals in the name of Christ and the fellowship of his church through any crucial decision in relationships or during any crisis in life.

First, we can expect an increase in the effectiveness of our ministry to people during periods of stress. We will know more of who needs what kind of help and who can assist them. This will occur because we have made a survey of needs, classified signs of growth and distress, enlisted and trained lay people as ministers, and cooperated with specialists in other helping agencies.

Second, we can expect some change in the actions and attitudes of our people toward the world and toward people in trouble, if we are willing to become organizers and implementers of service, apt teachers, and occasional counselors.

Third, we can expect to conserve our own energies. Priorities for service can be established. Alternatives to dependent relationships, including pastoral counseling, can be encouraged. There are agencies in the community with financial resources and trained personnel that can provide services which used to give ministers their significance. And there are competent church members who are willing to care for others, if we will recognize what they could or already may be doing. Why must we duplicate their efforts?

A program that leads to these goals would be

one that could be called "comprehensive" when:

1. the pastor works with those who care about others to provide a system of oversight for the entire congregation;

2. the church cooperates with other helping agencies to provide continuity of care for people in trouble (continuity means multiple types of service and a system for relating people from one service to another);

3. care-givers think of individuals in relation to the systems of our society—family, church, work, government—diagnose the way in which these systems contribute to the difficulties of a person, and work with these systems to provide more adequate support for troubled people.

CHAPTER TWO

Categories
for Caring

I heartily agree with your emphasis upon training pastors to be more skillful instead of encouraging pastors to leave the parish ministry for another occupation which allows them to practice the simpler or more specialized helper roles. We are beginning to discover here [Institute for Advanced Pastoral Studies] ministers who are highly skilled and who wish to remain as parish ministers. It seems to me in many ways that is the way of the future and a career decision much to be nurtured and encouraged.[1]

The skills of a minister begin with conceptual ability. This ability is what makes the minister a "professional." He or she is sensitive to many movements of people, a variety of nuances, and meanings in words. But the minister is not confused by all these stimuli because he or she has a framework for extracting what is most significant for helping people. Also, the minister can interpret

---

[1] Jack Birsdorf, director, Institute for Advanced Pastoral Studies, personal correspondence, August 12, 1974.

what is seen and heard in words and attitudes that make sense to those who seek his or her counsel.

Systematic thinking about people is the first step toward handling the many demands that are made upon a pastor. Our model is the thinking processes of our Lord revealed in the Gospels. We add to this, from a human point of view, the resources of modern survey methods. From the general sociological questionnaire we learn more about all the flock, and from personal assessment kits we quickly find the locus of difficulty in an individual. With these aids to our ministry, we can know what is in the hearts of those who seek our guidance. We also have a method for ordering the priorities of our own time and deciding who needs to see us and who would be served better by either a lay leader or a specialized counselor. And a systematic way of viewing the needs of people will aid lay ministers in the evaluation of their own contacts. When the results of a year's ministry are tabulated, church leaders will know the types of growth or stress experienced by members of the congregation. We will have a more personal view of the body of Christ under our care.

In the long run, our ministry will be more convincing because we will know where people really are in their hopes and fears, triumphs and discouragements.

Jesus Knew People

Jesus was convincing because he knew the hearts of men (John 2:25). This was more than a general awareness of the ways that people thought about him and God. It was also a penetrating assessment of the thoughts and ways of an individual. Early in his ministry he judged Nathanael to be an open and honest person, one who was willing to raise questions and to accept the answers of one who could satisfy his desire for truth (John 1:47). Jesus immediately saw that Peter had qualities which could be firmed up as a foundation for church organization (John 1:42, Matthew 16:18, Acts 11:14).

When people were spiritually burdened and physically handicapped, Jesus could decide on which was the greater need of the person. The man who was sick from palsy needed something more than relief from physical suffering (Matthew 9:2).

Could we follow the example of our Lord? We could not have his divine omniscience (John 16:30), but we could learn to observe people as closely as he did and develop his art of asking questions. In the midst of trying circumstances, as when he came down from the Mount of Transfiguration to find his disciples without faith, he could still ask the troubled father of a sick boy how long he had been troubled with this disease (Mark 9:21). In the midst of grief, he could ask sensible and factual questions, such as, "Where have you laid him?" (John 11:34). When a blind man kept yelling at him in a crowd, Jesus could penetrate through the confusion of the mob with a question for action, "What do you want me to do for you?" (Luke 18:41).

His questions were not only for purposes of information, but also they formed a bridge for communication. When he found Mary Magdalene grieving at the empty tomb, he asked the reason for her weeping (John 20:15). Gradually he led her to an awareness of the marvelous event that transformed his relationship to her and to every earthly person.

The art of inquiry in Jesus can be seen not only in his questions, but also in his leading statements. The conversation with the woman at the well (John 4) could have been a series of intersecting monologues between an opinionated Samaritan and a defensive Jew. But Jesus treated each statement by the woman as an opportunity to make a reply that intrigued her curiosity and led her toward a deeper awareness of herself and God. The results of that conversation should be coveted by every pastor: she knew herself, she had found the godly goal for her life, and she told the Good News to her neighbors.

Although the disciples were amazed at the powers of observation and knowledge of inner thoughts that appeared in Jesus, he was not content with a series of individualized insights. He went beyond this to order his insights into general classifications. These were presented in his parables. The story of the sower taught his disciples to consider the personality structure and the social environment of those to whom they preached. Both the background and the present condition of a person would have much to do with one's receptiveness and steadfastness to the kingdom of God (Luke 8:4-15).

Think Before You Act

What are the general principles from Jesus' way of thinking about people that will aid our pastoral ministry?

First, he was an acute observer. He saw people as they were, where they were. He combined a penetration into the hearts of individuals with a wide awareness of what was going on around him. A woman could not even touch his garment in a crowd without his knowing that virtue had gone out of him. In the midst of the bedlam of a departure from Jericho, he could hear the plaintive call of a blind man. Busy as he was with his teaching of the disciples, he saw those who had brought little children and made a place for them.

Out of a wide range of awareness, Jesus could pick the people who were important, the events that were significant, and the time when people were ready to hear or were anxious for help. This is the realistic base for any system of pastoral care: a continual openness to what is going on around us and discriminating judgment as to what is most significant for our relationship with that person or event.

If we are going to help people, we must select out of all their responses the clues to conditions that we are trained to observe, classify, and treat. We may not be the persons who will offer a specific remedy, but we should be able to identify the area of difficulty. We are not expected to provide specialized diagnoses as would be found in medicine or a subspecialty such as psychiatry. As was shown by a nationwide survey in 1960, people do not come to ministers when they know that they have some specific and deep-seated emotional problem. But they do come when they are generally anxious and cannot locate the source of their difficulty. We are expected to know enough about human nature to identify the area of difficulty and assess motivation and goals for life.

This is possible if we can follow a second principle, which is to arrange our selected observations under several general categories. That is, we manage what we learn by sorting out the facts in some systematic way. Jesus began this process by graphic portrayals of the various conditions of people who would hear the gospel. The apostle Paul continued the practice in his "household sayings." The longest of these, in his letter to the Ephesians, discusses the manifestations of the Christian life in the neighborhood, work, family, church, inner thoughts, and character. His classification of areas of living would be similar to the "diagnostic kit" which was developed in the sixties at the Bradley Psychiatric Center for use by ministers and doctors.

Classification is a foundation stone for the third characteristic of Jesus' way of thinking. He consistently showed the relationship between attitude and act, described the deeper spiritual and psychological meaning of some commonplace event. When, for example, he stood with his disciples before the temple treasury, they saw nothing unusual. But he singled out the obscure action of a widow as the dramatic sacrifice of one who would receive greater glory from God than the rich with their noisy almsgiving. When the people sought to make him a king, he knew their actions were motivated by nothing more than a desire for physical comfort.

This ability to interpret the deeper meaning of an action was the characteristic of Jesus' temptation experience. As Matthew reported this (chapter 4), Jesus met every request for action with a comment on the significance of such an action for his relationship with God or the Devil. He was not deceived, because he could connect the outward movement with a desired motivation.

This third characteristic of Jesus' thinking is one of the most helpful characteristics of a mature spiritual guide. It is a characteristic that Dr. Irvin Yalom and his associates found in a study of encounter groups among college students. The group that made the most progress was led by a group leader who served as an interpreter of attitudes, who showed the relationship between action and attitude or one attitude and another. In contrast, leaders who only reflected back what was said in the group, or who tried to move the group on the basis of their own charm and influence, provided less help for the participants.[2]

The actions of Jesus were based upon this analytic way of thinking. He saw clearly what was in a person because he was an accurate observer, classifier, and interpreter.

Helps for Human Analysis

We can model our thinking after that of Jesus, but only if we recognize our limitations. We need

[2]Morton A. Lieberman, Irvin D. Yalom, and Matthew B. Miles, "Encounter: The Leader Makes the Difference," *Psychology Today,* vol. 6, no. 10 (March, 1973), pp. 74-76.

some procedures that will increase our awareness of what is going on, compare our system of classification with those of others, and provide some means of controlling our conclusions. A partial answer to these problems comes through development of spiritual and psychological maturity, and through professional training. Another aid comes from the fields of psychology and sociology, which have developed the social survey, the personal interview, professional consultation, and group consensus. Each of these methods assists the pastor and other church leaders to know people more accurately than would be possible by subjective judgments. We will have a more reliable picture of an individual and a more realistic ministry to that person when we recognize our own limitations and use the professional aids that are becoming available to us.

Church and Community Surveys

If we are going to help people where they are, we must know the conditions of their life and the resources that are readily available to them. We can obtain some of this information through our own walks and talks in the community. But we can also check our findings by more systematic surveys, which may have already been conducted by some community agency or sponsored by a denomination.

City managers and area planning councils will usually have studies of socioeconomic conditions of a community which are readily available to a pastor or other civic leaders. These surveys have been mandatory for communities that wished to receive federal funds for a variety of projects. In addition to the local surveys of a city or county, there often are regional surveys, such as the Ford Foundation study of Appalachia.

In addition to general community surveys, specific agencies will often conduct studies for their own purposes, such as the Health Opinion Survey, which was conducted by the Community Psychiatry Division, University of North Carolina, in several rural counties.[3]

In the church, surveys can give us a general picture of the congregation and the opinions, attitudes, and activities of a special group, such as youth. An example is Church Youth Research, established by Merton Strommen, Minneapolis, Minnesota.[4] Questions were developed from a nationwide survey of church youth and placed in a questionnaire that was mailed to all of the young

[3]The survey may be ordered for $1.50 from the Division of Community Psychiatry, University of North Carolina, Chapel Hill, NC 27514.

[4]Information on the surveys can be obtained from Dr. Merton Strommen, 122 West Franklin Street, Minneapolis, MN 55404.

people in a specific congregation. The question-naires are to be returned confidentially to Minneapolis and tabulated by electronic equipment so that the final report will show relationships between (1) what bothers youth the most; (2) what they do believe; (3) what is important to them; and (4) what their attitudes are toward other young people in the church and toward guidance provided by church leaders and others. As data has been accumulated from a large number of churches of various denominations, the research center is able to provide the young people and their leaders with (1) a comparison of the scores of each young person with those of all young persons in the congregation; (2) a comparison between the cumulative scores of all the young persons in the congregation and those of other young persons of the same denomination; (3) and a comparison of the scores of young people of various ages in a church with the scores of adults in the same congregation. These scores often reveal, for example, that the adults are greatly concerned about parental understanding, the dating problems of young people, and moral problems. Senior students show less concern than adults in almost all areas and give more emphasis to their relationships to teachers and less emphasis to moral problems.

The research center sends out an analysis of each score. For example, the report will show that a youth who scores high on concern for family relationships is probably troubled about his or her relationships with other people as well. The highest scores are from youth whose parents are separated or divorced. A youth who would score low on family relationship concerns would come from a devout family which was free from financial worry.

Surveys of this type will not only increase the range and reliability of the pastor's assessment of individuals, church, and community, but they will also reduce the pressure upon a minister to make evaluations single-handedly and to use personal authority or prestige as a basis for program implementation. With the aid of research services, the clergy and church members have an objective evaluation of their condition.

Psychological Interviews

Sociological surveys aid the minister to approximate the first characteristic of Jesus' thinking about people, which was a broad range of awareness. Psychological interviews aid the pastor in imitation of Jesus' depth of perspective and ability to describe what was really happening in a person.

It is possible to use a type of interview that will not only save time for the pastor and those who seek help, but will also develop stronger relationships with other professionals in the community. An example of this combination is the training program and mental health assessment kit developed by the Bradley Center in Columbus, Georgia.

In the 1960s, the mental health staff of the Bradley Center began to train ministers and doctors in the use of a questionnaire that would evaluate an individual's overall adjustments, pinpoint areas of special stress and conflict, and formulate questions necessary to supplement the available data. The questionnaire could be completed by an individual in little more than an hour and scored by a pastor or physician in fifteen minutes to half an hour. When completed, the pastor would know the major area of difficulty and the severity of trouble experienced by an individual. The ministers were so delighted at the time saved by this method that one of them characterized the feeling of awe when he said, "These methods permit me to start counseling at the point where I used to stop!"[5]

In four hours of seminars, ministers and physicians learned how to score the answers to questions and make statements or ask questions of their clients that would lead toward better understanding of problems and a resolution of con-

[5]David Shapiro and Leonard Maholick, *Opening Doors for Troubled People* (Springfield, Ill.: Charles C. Thomas, Publisher, 1963), p. 56.

flicts. In addition, clergy and physicians attended two-hour weekly workshops until they were proficient in handling the assessment methods. At these workshops, each person gave some examples of his or her work and received comments from the mental health staff and other members of that person's own profession. The first group of ministers met weekly for four months and then came into the Center for periodic consultation on their cases. Through this training these people were enabled to evaluate more accurately the needs of those seeking help.

In addition to the confidence that came from consultation in the mental health center, ministers found that they could work with physicians in the training program in the care of their people. For example, a teenager was so terrified at going out of the house and was so anxious about everything she touched that she would not go with her minister to receive help in the mental health center. When the pastor sought the aid of the family physician, who was in the training program with him, the young lady responded to the physician's reassurances and was taken to the center.

The areas assessed in the questionnaire are: occupation, schooling, relationship with parents, marriage, relationship with children, religion, and social-cultural-recreational activities. Questions are also asked on economic status and physical health.[6]

Judging by the Fruit

When we have completed surveys, evaluated our findings with research consultants, and discussed conclusions with other church leaders, will we really know the hearts of men as Jesus knew them? No, we will not. We look on the outward appearance and only God looks into the heart. It was for this reason that Jesus instructed his disciples to judge people by their fruits. As we observe conduct, we get some clue to character. The fruit that Jesus looked for was the result of repentance: love, justice, mercy. He did not measure people by the superficial styles of his day. He looked for the fruit of that which came directly from the heart rather than for conduct that was imposed by the regulations of people. To know people by their fruits is to see evidence of the direction in which they are moving. We judge them to be either productive or unproductive (Matthew 13:8), useful or difficult (Matthew 7:16).

A pastoral classification should be built upon a person's sense of direction. This is not only obedience to the Master's observations, but is also

[6]All of the materials in the Personal Data Kit except the Cornell Index are included in *The Mental Health Counselor in the Community* by David S. Shapiro, Leonard Maholick, Fail Brewer, and Richard Robertson (Springfield, Ill.: Charles C. Thomas, Publisher, 1968).

the most productive approach to classification. We use a classification as a signpost, a way of saying to ourselves and others that a person is headed in one direction or another, at a fast or slow pace.

But how are we going to judge directions? A pastor would start with a person's relationship to God and to the church. A physician would start with the relationships between the eight different systems of the body. An analyst would relate ego to id and superego. A mental health worker would measure the adaptation of the individual to family and society. Each profession adopts a system of classification that identifies the goals of our work.

The categories for classification are embedded in a number of biblical passages. Galatians 5 contains a catalog of the works of the flesh and the fruit of the spirit. In chapter 25 of Matthew, Jesus enumerates the types of troubles that should be met by Christian action. Ezekiel, chapter 34, proclaims the activities of adequate shepherds toward the lost, the stray, the crippled, the weak, the strong. Each of these groups must be "fed in justice." In modern terms we would say that a pastor and other church leaders must distribute their time and attention to the healthy, the worried healthy, the early sick, the intermittently ill, and the chronic sufferers.

What categories can we derive from biblical sources that will be productive for our work?

A classification that meets some of these qualifications was recommended by Anton Boisen in *Problems in Religion and Life.*[7] He later reported the use of this classification in a village survey by a pastor who had once studied with him. The 322 persons in the survey were divided into the following categories: the faithful (52), the complacent (more than half), the pagan (29), the mentally ill (81), the reorganized (4).[8]

I revised this classification when I was pastor of a surburban congregation. During my first year I visited each home or had some personal contact with 75 percent of the 190 homes in the church membership. I grouped the two hundred persons to whom I talked privately into the following categories:

Classification	Number of Persons	Percentage of Total
Prospects	43	21%
The growing	25	13%
The faithful	21	10%
The careless	10	5%
The distressed	77	39%
The isolated	12	6%

[7]Anton T. Boisen, *Problems in Religion and Life* (Nashville: Abingdon Press, 1946), pp. 36-37.
[8]Anton T. Boisen, *Religion in Crisis and Custom* (New York: Harper & Row, Publishers, 1955), pp. 22-32.

1. Prospects. The basic intention of my visit to persons in this category was to effect a profession of faith or active church membership. From conversations with these persons I found that many of them could also be classified under "distressed." I chose to place them first in the prospect category because the goal of Christian discipleship takes priority over all others in the church's ministry.

When a prospect has made a profession of faith or become an active church member, he or she may be placed in the next classification, "the growing," or "the distressed," or "the isolated." The last category may sound strange, but there are occasions when a new convert is still unacceptable in a congregation. One of the advantages of a pastoral classification is to keep up with the movement of a person within the fellowship of a church. In addition, reclassification assumes a continuity of pastoral care. The individual continues to be our concern.

2. The Growing. This group includes new church members, children who have been through a pastor's class and are voting members of the congregation, young people, engaged couples, newlyweds, and new parents. The objective for this group would be similar to the first two emphases of American Baptists, who were asked in 1961 to state the reasons for church membership. The first was "in helping me to know of God's love and care for me in strengthening my faith." The second was "in broadening my understanding of the meaning of life."[9] A similar objective was very important to members of the United Church of Christ, as stated in a 1968 survey: "The church should help me provide proper Christian education for my children (86%), strengthen my faith and religious devotion (58.3%), build good moral foundations for my personal life (49.6%)."[10]

One of the most delightful parts of this classification is the movement into it by middle-aged persons who have previously been grouped as "careless," "distressed," or "isolated." The objectives stated by the American Baptist and United Church of Christ members can be achieved as people move through a crisis or a crucial period of life. When this happens, we need some institutional evidence of change. Reclassification is a reminder to pastors that certain people are no longer to be seen as "problems." When the pastor gives a periodic summary of ministry to the church leadership, a shift in percentages from distressed, isolated, and careless into growing or faithful would be a significant indicator

---

[9] *The American Baptist, His Mission, Message and Church,* prepared by Harvey A. Everett and Isaac Igarashi (New York: American Baptist Home Mission Societies, 1961), p. 26.

[10] Victor Obenhaus, *And See the People* (Chicago: Chicago Theological Seminary, 1968), p. 13.

that some basic purposes of church membership were being achieved.

3. The Faithful. The faithful members meet two criteria. First, they are regular and responsible in church work. Second, they are not suffering at the present time from any of the problems that would place them in the "distressed" group. As we will see, many persons who are faithful to the church are classified under "distressed" because this is the primary reason for pastoral attention.

Although pastors have many organizational contacts with persons in this category, they are often neglected as persons. When I visited these families on a routine basis, I was often told that this was the first time a minister had come to the home without some plan to get them involved in a church program or because there was some emergency. Several deacons and their wives said that a pastor had never been in their home or that they had never sat down with a minister for half an hour to an hour to just talk about themselves and their religious life.

These people are the core of any ministering fellowship. They are not overburdened with problems, and they have a sense of mission. If a pastor will pay attention to them, they will take heed with the pastor to the rest of the flock.

4. The Careless. In contrast, 5 percent of the congregation was both indifferent to the church and unaware of any personal problems. This group was part of the group that sociologists call "nominal" Protestants. They may have their names on a church roll and attend church once or twice a year. I found some of these people to be hostile to a particular pastor or church member, but most of them felt neither love nor hate for a particular church organization, its activities, or beliefs.

The attribute of "careless" did not mean that these people were careless about their own family life or their responsibilities in the community. Some of them were my valuable allies in understanding the community, planning civic activities, or guiding church members toward sources of help.

5. The Distressed. The largest portion of counseling and visitation during the first year was to distressed persons. Most of these people were seen at home or at the church.

The varieties of distress were:

Physically ill	23
Emotionally ill	19
Bereaved	11
Aged and lonely	11
Husband-wife conflict	9
Parent-child problem	2
Alcoholism	2

A more established clergyperson would probably

have seen more persons with husband-wife and parent-child conflicts. In the 1960 field study by the Survey Research Center, thirty-four clergymen listed the following types of problems that were handled by counseling during one year.[11]

	Percentage of Total
Marital	58.7 %
Child-parent	9.2 %
Juvenile behavior problems	8 %
Problems of the aged	7.2 %
Mental-emotional	6.8 %
Alcoholism	3.9 %
Other	6.2 %

6. *The Isolated.* I met people in this category as a new pastor. They were returning to the church because of different leadership, but they either felt rejection from the older members or they had some continuing hostility toward some who were dominant in the present leadership.

The isolation might also be sociological, as in the case of a laborer who was ashamed to drive his family to church in a pickup truck, their only source of transportation.

[11]Reginald Robinson, David F. DeMarche, and Mildred K. Wagle, *Community Resources in Mental Health* (New York: Basic Books, Inc., Publishers, 1960), p. 242.

Some isolation was physical, such as the physically handicapped person who lacked transportation to church but who still had some contacts with the membership and was not suffering physical or psychological anguish.

Counting the Cost

Jesus cautioned his disciples to count the cost of discipleship, just as a wise man considers the expense of a tower before he builds it. We can apply this wisdom to a program of pastoral care. We must first know the needs of the congregation before we can determine the type of program that is necessary to meet those needs. For the pastors, there must not only be some long-range planning and training of members for ministry, but there must also be some method by which to set priorities for visitation, decide when to spend their own time or send others, develop a reporting system to church leaders so they can guide, and confirm the pastors in the use of energy with various types of people in church and community. Some classification is a precondition of planning and management of comprehensive care.

CHAPTER THREE

Why Programs Succeed

When John Oman, pastor of Wesley United Methodist Church in downtown Minneapolis, began training sessions for lay people who were to conduct group counseling in the church, he looked for biblical guidance[1] in the statement of the apostle Paul, "Therefore encourage one another and build one another up . . ." (1 Thessalonians 5:11). The functions of such a ministry were again summarized in 1 Corinthians 14:40, where Paul writes, "admonish the idle, encourage the fainthearted, help the weak, be patient with them all."

The Wesley program began with a dinner meeting of "decision-makers" suggested by the chairman of the board or church council. The pastor met weekly for six weeks with this group to discuss dynamics and principles of group counseling. During this time

[1]John B. Oman, *Group Counseling in the Church* (Minneapolis: Augsburg Publishing House, 1972), p. 11.

the members were divided into groups of five or six and the lay counseling leadership rose to the surface through these mini-group counseling sessions.

The decision-makers were enthusiastic for the development of this type of ministry throughout the church. They were reassured that the cost would be no more than the one dollar each person contributed during each counseling session to pay for literature and guest speakers. The program would not be a budgeted church item.

An advisory board was chosen to direct the program and approve selection of group leaders. The pastor interviewed all possible group leaders, and those who would follow a problem-solving approach to group work were asked to become part of one group for a year. During this year, each prospective leader rotated among several groups. In a monthly meeting of group leaders, the rising group of leaders was evaluated as being sarcastic, suspicious, friendly, or creative.

As Pastor Oman reflected on the development of these groups, he found that this "priesthood of believers" allowed him to prepare and preach a sermon, visit the sick, officiate at weddings and funerals, and attend to the administrative functions of the church. Without them, he would have been deluged by people in trouble. As a counseling pastor, he saw at least twenty persons a week. Since it was seldom possible to solve a problem in one interview, he would have had twenty in one week, plus twenty the next week—where would it end? The answer was referral to group leaders.

Two Movements Toward Lay Ministries

The Wesley program of Pastor Oman represents one development toward lay ministries. It is an emphasis upon small group discussions which are generally associated with "renewal" in the church or the "human potential" movement in society. Whether the program begins in a church, such as the Church of the Savior in Washington, D.C., or as an association of laymen, such as Yokefellows, ministers act more as coaches, and lay leaders are prominent in organization and group work.

The Small Group

How are these group ministries related to pastoral ministries?

The first groups after World War II were more than pastoral—they were psychiatric. At the Religio-Psychiatric Clinic of Marble Collegiate Church in New York City, group therapy was organized for persons who were assumed to have long-term neuroses, or who had severe emotional disturbances that required some psychiatric staff attention in the clinic. The promotion of this part of the Collegiate program by the pastor, Norman Vincent Peale, gave many persons the impression that a group program was only for sick people.

In developing the Wesley program, John Oman had to make clear the distinction between psychiatric group therapy, which required professional leadership, and group counseling in a church setting, which was for the rank and file of problem-burdened people who sought a clergyperson for counsel.[2]

In the fifties and sixties, group fellowship became better known as a specifically Christian movement for the expression of faith and personal renewal. This was the second form of group work which was popularized by Elton Trueblood and Samuel Shoemaker. The special contribution of this emphasis was the lay ministry. By 1964 there were enough lay academies and retreat centers in Europe and the United States for Olive Wyon to publish *Centres of Renewal* (Geneva: World Council of Churches).

This "renewal" emphasis was upon personal and institutional development. It was thought that as individuals were inspired through the fellowship of a small group, they would contribute to the

[2]*Ibid*, p. 16.

development of new forms for church growth that would meet personal needs.

A third relationship of group work to pastoral ministries came in the sixties when "marriage enrichment" seminars grew in popularity. Some of these, like the usual "human potential" seminars, concentrated exclusively upon problems presented by the persons who enrolled for a series of sessions or a weekend meeting of twelve to twenty-four hours. The *Atlanta Constitution* featured a marriage encounter program held at Ignatius House, a Catholic retreat which welcomes all religions. During a weekend, couples who thought that their marriage was "perfect" discovered some new skills in communicating. There were discussions about debt, sex, money, and what society thinks marriage should be. Spouses kept notebooks of their thoughts and traded them for discussion. The session in a group was not like a "sensitivity" group with lots of sharing. The notebook of intimate thoughts was seen only by the mate.[3]

Training for Church Officers

Another development of lay ministries has come through denominationally sponsored emphasis

[3]"Perfect Marriage? Guess Again," *Atlanta Constitution*, August 18, 1974.

upon the training of church officers for a variety of tasks, including pastoral ministries. Some of this direction may be attributed to the success of the small group movement in churches, where lay leaders demonstrated sensitivity to individuals and perseverance in the maintenance of an organization.

The training of church officers may arise out of dissatisfaction with their participation in the life of the church, or the need of the pastor for help with his duties, or both. In a county-seat town, the pastor of a 1,400 member church, Jerry Songer, felt that deacons should be more active. A Yokefellow program was developed in which each deacon and a partner ministered to twenty-two families of the congregation. This was the deacon's "sheepfold." The deacons and their partners also attended six seminars on church doctrine and organization, pastoral ministries, and evangelism.

Approximately two-thirds of the deacons participated in the seminars and visited church members to enlist them in a program of regular prayer in each family. Although the deacons considered the seminars to be somewhat academic, they reported a wide range of problems for which they tried to provide some answers:

Benevolence: A deacon arranged for unused food from a local drive-in to go to an indigent nursing home; another assisted a father in negotiating with creditors; a third provided groceries for a widow.

Shut-ins: The visits were so rewarding to the deacons that a weekly visitation program was organized.

Illness: Deacons visited persons during terminal illnesses and went back to see the families when death occurred. When a church call for a minister could not be answered, a deacon made the visit to a man in critical condition.

Transients: This involved location of overnight facilities, brief hospitalization, and counsel with drug addicts.

Young people: Discussions were held with a pregnant young girl and her grandmother, with whom she lived; also with a runaway girl; and help was given in the reconciliation of a boy with foster parents.

Marriage: Assistance toward remarriage was given to a widower, and advice to an estranged couple.

Aged: Transportation for worship services was provided, refreshments served, and worship services in homes were arranged.

Troubled: Discussions were held in jail, sometimes in the early morning hours, or in homes, with persons considering suicide, divorce,

or who showed symptoms of being psychotic.
Witnessing: Deacons reported a variety of conversations to unchurched or unsaved persons, with a high percentage of the unchurched deciding to join or attend church.[4]

The Combination of Emphases

Pastoral care may become the focus of lay ministry-group programs. It is natural for these emphases to be combined. Both are based on program responsibilities by church leaders and utilize group techniques. The outreach of both is through individual contacts which may lead to the commitment of a new person to a group in the church or a community organization.

The style of this combination may vary from an urban "company of the committed" to a small-town conventional church with evangelistic traditions.

An example of the former style is the Duke Street Baptist Church in Alexandria, Virginia. This middle class church had ninety members in 1974. Membership is renewed annually. Eighty-six percent of dwellings in the neighborhood are multiple family units.

A basic course in pastoral care is offered for

[4]Jerry Songer, "A Project: The Deacon Ministry" (submitted as partial requirement for the Doctor of Ministry degree, Southeastern Baptist Theological Seminary, 1974).

lay people over an eight-month period. All twenty of the deacons (men and women) are graduates of the course. It has been taught four times in five years. The primary aim is learning pastoral skills. The teaching method includes reports of visits made by lay people, discussion of the reports, lectures and demonstrations of techniques of interviewing, evaluating, communicating, and serving persons in need.

An advanced course for deacons is designed for continuing education and support of these persons who perform 90 percent of the pastoral care ministry of the church. The pastor serves as a teacher-consultant. Along with role playing and verbatim reports of visits, there is some emphasis upon communication difficulties among deacons, but no discussion of personal matters such as family or job. But, for example, when a deacon resigns (in this area near Washington, D.C., there are many transfers), there is a meeting for expression of grief and other feelings about the loss of this member.

A variety of feelings may be expressed in other groups: personal growth group, parent discussion group, marriage checkup and growth group, personal potential and achievement motivation group, dynamics of Christian relating group, and Bible study/personal growth group. Persons in these groups receive the opinions of others about their life and relational styles as they tell something personal.

For several years the pastor, James Fox, has met weekly with two men and two women who lead the Bible study and personal growth groups to discuss the interpersonal processes of these programs.

In a small-town setting, a similar process with less elaborate organization can be developed.

The Elements of Success

Why do these programs work well? Some of the twenty-five churches in my sample of observation, interviewing, and correspondence were studied as part of the Doctor of Ministry projects by their pastors. Through the use of questionnaires and interviews with church officers and members of the congregation, Kenneth E. Jones drew these conclusions from his training program at the First Christian Church, Borger, Texas: (1) The "Self-Anchoring Scale," administered before and after several months of training, showed increased self-confidence, involvement, and commitment on the part of thirty church officers in the course. (2) Congregational responses confirmed a previous hypothesis that the needs of individuals within the Christian community were being met more quickly and personally than before the training took place. There was more receptivity to ministry from church officers and a growing sense of "belonging" by the congregation. (3) Diaries kept by selected church officers and lay persons recorded actual instances and "felt" responses regarding their ability to be involved in situations such as death, illness, inactivity, and friendly concern. The ministry seemed to be valuable whether it was by phone or personal visit. (4) At the conclusion of the training, church officers said that they had "confidence to do things they always wanted to do, but had been afraid to try," were more aware of responsibility to "minister to persons where they are in life," and possessed a new feeling of "mutual concern" and inspiration from the group meetings and visitation program.[5]

Similar conclusions are reflected in studies by Eugene Tyre, Charles Howell, and Ted McCollum of "deacon-led" programs of ministry, although they found less change toward a pastoral role by deacons than they had hoped for.[6]

---

[5]Kenneth E. Jones, "Enabling Local Church Officers to Perform Ministry" (field project for Doctor of Ministry degree, Graduate Seminary of Phillips University, 1973), pp. 50-71.

[6]Eugene Tyre, "A Program to Equip the Diaconate of the First Baptist Church, Cartersville, Georgia, to Function as Ministers" (field project for Doctor of Ministry degree, Southern Baptist Theological Seminary, 1973), pp. 69-78; Ted McCollum, personal correspondence, October 7, 1974; Charles Howell, "Developing the Ministry of Believers at Parkway Baptist Church" (field project for Doctor of Ministry degree, Southeastern Baptist Theological Seminary, 1974).

Although there are no specific evaluations of other programs, there are some common themes which help us know the degree and type of pastoral care that will develop from a training program:

1. *Theological assumptions of the program meet lay expectations of the church as an institution.*

In a study of questionnaires from sixty-five churches of nine Protestant denominations, Philip Hammond found four images of the church among laymen:

a. Theocentric: God-centered and oriented toward community activity. The Duke Street Church program developed with a dual emphasis upon Bible study and ministry to the personal needs of transfer-prone apartment dwellers in a metropolitan suburb.

b. Sociocentric: Not God-centered, but involved in community activity. None of the churches in my sample would include this expectation.

c. Egocentric: Not God-centered, nor community-centered. The church is considered to be a secular organization designed primarily to benefit its own members on an individual basis. A program to counteract this emphasis was developed by Robert Van House. In a United Methodist church, he led a three-month learning experience for the church's Council on Ministries that would develop "participative style of leadership." The content was Wesley's doctrine of man as a social being, responsible personally to God and to his neighbor. "Perfection" was seen not as individual search for righteousness, but as participation with others in building up the body of Christ. Along with this content there was discussion of feelings about leadership and the sharing of responsibility in this particular church.[7]

d. Ecclesia-centric: God-oriented,   sacred organization designed primarily to benefit its own members but not the larger community.[8] The "deacon-led" programs begin with this orientation but usually contain some community contacts with health and welfare agencies.

When there is agreement between purposes of the pastoral training and expectations of participants, evaluation questionnaires contain positive comments like, "One of the most valuable things that came out of our Church Officer training was the confidence to do things I have always wanted to do, but been afraid to try."[9]

---

[7]Robert Van House, "The Wesleyan Doctrine of Man and Leadership Practice in a United Methodist Church" (field project, Doctor of Ministry degree, Graduate Seminary of Phillips University, 1974).

[8]For examples of these categories, see Philip E. Hammond, "The Role of Ideology in Church Participation" (Ph.D. thesis, Columbia University, 1960).

[9]Jones, *op. cit.,* p. 63.

2. *The congregation developed a preference for a designated church officer as its primary pastor.*

In the First Christian Church of Borger, the congregation was divided into "ranges" of thirty families and several "ranches" under each range. From a before-after congregational survey, the pastor found that a large majority of the people, after they had been visited by their deacon, would prefer to share a serious problem with him rather than with a fellow church member, which had been their first preference before the program began.[10] A ministry to members was considered to be a major task for church officers.

The congregational survey of First Baptist Church, Baxley, Georgia, contained a 90 percent affirmation of a family-care ministry by deacons. A 10 percent negation came from persons who rejected the concept of the deacon's role as that of a pastoral minister or who had not been visited by a deacon.[11]

Some pastors expressed disappointment at the superficial nature of some church officer contacts. This was attributed to the nature of small towns, where people knew each other well and would not share much with someone from the church. I would

---

[10]*Ibid.,* p. 56.
[11]Ted McCollum, personal correspondence, October 7, 1974.

suggest that this is not always the case.

3. *Members of the congregation, and others, respond with warmth and understanding to relationships with church officers who have been through a training period that evoked warmth, insight, and honesty, or who were chosen for those qualities.*

Duke Street Church and other Church of the Savior type churches are obvious examples of relationship-style organizations. Deacons at Duke Street were also members of interpersonal relation groups. In the Wesley church, leaders for ministry arose from group counseling sessions over the period of a year. Those who demonstrated qualities of empathy and understanding became the designated pastors for others.

What happens in churches where leaders are chosen for community status or zeal for administration? Several of the questionnaire summaries from congregations and officers contain demands for all new deacons to receive training in ministry. Officers who dislike this duty, or who cannot schedule visits, probably are among the fourth to a third of officers who did not attend the courses on preparation for pastoral care. The new and the old could continue with a plan that emerged from the training of deacons at First Baptist Church in Cartersville, Georgia. Deacons would be given a choice of committees: administration, ministry to the unchurched, ministry to the church, and community ministries. Pastoral ministries would become an expected service by many church leaders without requiring that all leaders elect this type of church responsibility.

As interest increases in the pastoral qualities of church leaders, we can ask why some men and women emerge as "natural" group leaders, or why, as John Ackerman found in a program at St. Elizabeth's Hospital, Washington, D.C., that lay people learn as much as, if not more than, ministers in identical courses on pastoral care and counseling.[12]

A preliminary answer may be found in a study of the biographies of young staff members who were reassuring to schizophrenic patients. All but one of the young people came from problem families, sometimes including an alcoholic father or a psychotic mother.

Psychiatrists reading the staff's autobiographies might well predict serious psychological problems for many of them. Instead, our staff seem to be examples of

---

[12] John Ackerman, personal correspondence October 1, 1974; also, research on professional vs. nonprofessional therapy is summarized by Joseph A. Durlak, "Myths Concerning the Nonprofessional Therapist," *Professional Psychology*, vol. 4, no. 3 (August, 1973), pp. 300-304.

invulnerable children raised in difficult situations.[13]

The young people were not as intimately intertwined with a psychopathologic parent as was a brother or sister, usually older. The healthy young person served as a neutral caretaker for the parent.

The senior staff believed that these young "caretakers" could relate to disturbed people more easily than highly trained mental health professionals who often gave intellectual responses when a more "visceral" reaction would have been appropriate.

Future study may show some of the same contrasts between clergy, whom Jim Dittes has characterized as "little adults," and church leaders who were not overanxious about adult approval in earlier years and who have not inhibited their natural reactions to people in distress through professional training.[14] The ease with which such church leaders relate to people in need may explain increases in congregational expectations for more personal ministry from lay leaders.

[13] Loren Mosher, Ann Reifman, and Alma Menn, "Characteristics of Nonprofessionals Serving as Primary Therapists for Acute Schizophrenics," *Hospital and Community Psychiatry* (June, 1973), p. 394.

[14] See James Dittes, "Psychological Characteristics of Religious Professionals," in *Research in Religious Development,* ed. Merton Strommen (New York: Hawthorn Books Inc., 1971), p. 429.

4. *The permanence and penetration of lay ministries into the life of the church will depend upon the structuring of this emphasis into the continuing program of the church and the investment of personnel and/or budget into the more complex ministries of churches with more than a thousand active members.*

This finding has several facets:

a. Continuing lay ministries receive clergy support and official church sanction. There is a general expectation that these people represent the pastoral dimension of church life and that the pastor continually refers to them the majority of crucial or routine requests that come to his attention. One pastor, who now has an extensive program of lay ministry, said that in a previous church the people were interested, but the professional staff would not allow lay people to minister. Home and hospital visitation was a jealously guarded activity of associate pastors. (Sometimes the reverse is true, and the senior minister is *the* pastor.)

b. When a larger congregation is organized for group and individual ministry through lay leaders, a lay coordinator must be employed to:

coordinate program efforts, such as arranging schedules for meetings, supervising the flow of information about new members and others to designated deacons or "ranchers" (as in Borger);

maintain records and provide periodic reports to leaders and the pastor for purposes of maintaining existing responsibilities, developing new approaches, evaluating goals and objectives;

assist new leaders in assessing needs for their work, defining solutions to organizational problems, and getting the work started;

maintain the schedule of speakers and consultants for training programs of lay ministers. These characteristics are drawn from the specifications developed for lay coordinators of community programs in the North Carolina mental health program and the discipleship program of First Baptist Church, Norcross, Georgia.

c. A covenant of trust and responsibility must develop between pastor and lay leaders, between lay leaders, and between leaders and people who are served. There may be official announcements of requirements for personal growth groups, as in the Duke Street Baptist Church. Persons in these groups are expected to contribute to the financial support of the church or be confronted in the group. Confidentiality and faithful attendance are expected. Reports on visits or groups are expected in regular meetings of pastor and church officials.

5. *Lay ministries grow as clergy become resource*

persons rather than task-oriented managers, and lay leaders provide support for the clergyperson as a coach and accept pastoral responsibilities.

This reinforcing relationship was explicitly identified by the twenty-three groups of church leaders and pastors who met for a year in "Project Laity." Clergy were able in many instances to move toward an "enabling" role because of the emotional support and encouragement of group members. When the pastor was rigid about his traditional role, or when dominant group members inhibited change, the groups terminated.[15]

Pastors can often encourage the development of trust and support through retreats for church leaders that place personal sharing in the context of biblical and theological values. Pastor Tom Conley used group exercises like this:

Let's go around the circle and say in two sentences how Simon Peter is a part of me:
as I understand the meaning of faith
(Matthew 16:13-20)
when my violence comes out clearly
(John 18:10)
when I am frightened
(Matthew 26:69-75)

[15]Thomas Bennett, "Project Laity" (New York: National Council of Churches, 1961), pp. 43-44.

when I am most angry
   (Acts 8:20)
when I am prejudiced
   (Acts 10:9-16, 34-35)
when I'm tempted to go back to old sources
   of security
   (John 21).

We might ask ourselves the same questions, and
most especially the last one, when we see our people
encouraging one another without our immediate
help. It's so easy to desire the reassurance that
comes from someone who says how much *we* mean
to those who are distressed. But if we can find a new
source of security in a fellowship of committed
leaders who minister with us, we may find some of
the same satisfaction that came to Bill Self, pastor of
a large Atlanta church, when he made the following
call:

I had a terrible time with the traffic! Boy, was I
anxious—who would be there with Mrs. C. to
help her in the first shock of her husband's death?
And then I knew that I couldn't stay long because
I had to get back to the church for prayer meeting.

Well, when I finally got there, she was glad to
see me, and in a few minutes she was telling me
how much the visits of her deacon had meant to
her and her husband during his terminal hos-

pitalization. They had talked about death and what it meant to a Christian. I was most pleased with the deacon's ministry; it gave her a feeling that she wasn't alone in bearing her grief. But I had to leave her alone—she saw me looking at my watch and told me to go ahead; she knew that I had to get back to church. I was about to make some apologies when she saw Mr. R. walking into the yard. She almost shoved me out the door, saying, "Uh, it's all right, pastor. You can go now. My deacon is here."

CHAPTER FOUR

Ministry
Through Management

Comprehensive care is built upon the principles of participant management. The authorized leader expects a group of talented people to assume responsibility with him or her for the definition of organizational goals, planning of programs, implementation, control, and evaluation of objectives. Each person takes the lead in some area of work and may lead the entire group in some phases of the management process. The director is more of a coordinator than a doer of many things. He or she embodies the purpose of the agency, maintains its integrity, and arbitrates disagreements. Others take the credit—or blame—for work in specific parts of the program.

The spirit of participant management was expressed theologically in Paul's exhortation to the Corinthian church:

> What then is Apollos? What is Paul? Servants through whom you believed, as the Lord assigned to each. I planted, Apollos watered, but God gave the

growth. So neither he who plants nor he who waters is anything, but only God who gives the growth. He who plants and he who waters are equal, and each shall receive his wages according to his labor. For we are God's fellow workers; you are God's field, God's building.

1 Corinthians 3:5-9

Concentrating Concern for Caring

We strengthen the spirit and techniques of caring by asking these seven questions which identify the steps in participant management. The answers should be developed in cooperation with all of those who lead in the program.

1. *What is the mission of this church?* Discussions with church leaders and surveys like those mentioned in chapter 2 would provide advice and consent from the congregation for a ministry that would probably include the theological objectives listed in chapter 3. The pastor would have an articulated, approved theoretical basis for "motivation for ministry."

2. *What are the functions (activities) that express this mission?* A study committee composed of church leaders will usually come up with a list of activities that include visitation of members, support and advice to people in trouble, witnessing in the community. Here is an expression of what *this* church wishes to do. It will have to be modified or

strengthened by answers to the next question.

3. *What are our resources to perform these activities?* Now we get to the tenet that "every church member is a minister." The professional staff of any congregation is inadequate for a comprehensive program of visitation, group support, community cooperation in service to people in trouble. The resources will have to come from within the congregation and be hooked up with other organizations which supply other kinds of specialized assistance in the community.

4. *What duties should be assigned to whom?* In chapter 3 we reviewed two sources for lay ministry. These were the small group movement for Bible study or personal growth and training programs for church officers. Leaders for lay-ministry work in the congregation can be developed and trained through either of these kinds of programs to be "overseers" of part of the congregation.

5. *How much do we expect of the person to whom a duty is assigned?* First, there needs to be a parceling out of families in the church so that each "overseer" has a designated area of the city or number of families. Second, there should be some requirement, also made known to the congregation, that leaders will visit or call all persons under their care at some time in the next month. Sometimes there is a three-month buildup for every family

commitment to daily prayer or some other religious emphasis. Or the duty may be more general pastoral care, with some training for this ministry.

How well trained are group leaders or church officers for these responsibilities? The question of training depends upon the gap between resources and expectations. Does the church expect group leaders to be very competent in problem solving? Then they will need a year of training and supervision, as in Wesley Methodist, or the continuous supervision as in Duke Street Baptist.

Less intensive training would be expected for a "deacon-led" visitation program.

Whatever the degree of training, the important issue is to relate training to expectation, duties to responsibilities. This is the function of step-by-step planning and ratification of programs by the church—so that a lay minister knows what is expected, who has sanctioned the duties, and how he or she is to perform them.

6. *How do people report on their activities?* Two types of reporting should be noted. One is the case study or verbatim required of each participant in several training programs. This practice offers both an excellent opportunity to know that the officers are doing something and a teaching device for all who are in a seminar. At the same time, this method is too cumbersome for continuous use. It is time-

consuming for those involved in the reporting and the findings are difficult to classify.

For the church, a classification such as that described in the last sections of chapter 2 would have several values. A high percentage of reports of service to the "careless," "distressed," or "isolated" might mean that the church was really broadening contacts to people in trouble. If so, a vital question is whether the "faithful" will accept some of these troubled people into their organizations, and whether the church will create some organizations for those who are contacted, such as a fellowship group for divorcees, a teen club for delinquents, or a place for AA's to meet.

Another value of the classification is to see if there is a steady percentage of visits to "prospects," "growing," and "faithful." Pastoral care begins in earnest and concerned conversations with people before they have some crises. The establishment of normal, routine relationships is of great assistance when we must judge how a person will react during a crisis. Also, an established friendship means that we can do more during a crisis; our presence is an acknowledgment of tested care rather than the hurried visit of a stranger fulfilling an official duty. Furthermore, knowledge of an entire family during routine visits aids us when one person has trouble. A deacon who has the confidence of a father will be of real assistance to him and his son when the son gets into some trouble.

A reporting system also allows the pastor and his official board to know if the program of ministry is being maintained. There is expectation, training, and accountability. This leads inevitably to an opportunity for evaluation.

7. *What will be our measure of attainment of goals?* A classification system is basic to evaluation if it is built upon accepted goals of the organization. If we keep up the classification mentioned above, we will be able to record movement toward desirable goals. At the end of a year, inspection of records might show that 50 percent of the year's prospects and 25 percent of the careless were now classified as "growing" or "faithful." A decrease in the percentage of "isolated" or an increase in "faithful" would be an encouraging sign.

In addition to yearly summaries of routine classifications, an official board might request an in-depth inspection of religious commitment. Some useful criteria may be found in Morton King's survey of churches in Dallas, Texas: creedal assent and sense of personal commitment, participation in church activities, personal religious experience, personal ties in the congregation, commitment to intellectual search despite doubt, openness to religious growth, dogmatism, financial contributions, and talking and reading about religion.[1] The church might not want to use all the variables in Professor King's study, but the use of some of them could be compared with his study. More accurately, the use of some items one year could be compared with increases or decreases in these items in subsequent years in the same church. If the official board is wise enough to request electronic data processing of surveys (which can usually be arranged through denominational headquarters, local data-processing firms, or interested professors in universities), comparisons can be made between items. For example, what is the correlation, if any, between "personal ties in the congregation" and "financial contributions"?

As we move through these seven questions, or something like them, we gain consensus and form an organization. The steps need to be discussed with a planning committee or official board, tried out, reported on, and changed and approved by the church decision-making body. After approval, information should be given to the church and community so that lay ministers will move with security and authority in their tasks.

[1] Morton King, "Measuring the Religious Variable: Nine Proposed Dimensions," *Journal for the Scientific Study of Religion,* vol. 6, no. 2 (Fall, 1967), pp. 176-177.

Growth in Grace

The seven questions of participant management are similar to the questions that a person should ask when making any life decision. In planning a comprehensive program of pastoral care, the church leaders are training themselves as pastors, for they will use the same process with an organization and with an individual.

This combination of organization with personal care would have been theoretically impossible in the days when Herbert Simon's "scientific management" and Carl Rogers's "non-directive counseling" were dominant. Although both had valuable emphases, the scientific management cut the personal element out of administration, and the client-centered approach neglected structured decision making.

More recently, "organizational development" stresses group decision and individual satisfactions balanced with production needs. Organizational planning has been strongly influenced by Carl Rogers and Elton Mayo. At the same time, private health care organizations, like Kaiser Permanente, and government programs in physical and mental health have stressed the place of organization in delivery of help to individuals. Along with these powerful program incentives there has been a growth of research on the place of values and decision making in therapy.

It is now possible in theory as well as in practice to say that the way in which we structure relationships in our church will determine the way that members care for each other, and vice versa.

However, care must be taken to select and develop leaders who are willing to follow a compassionate and realistic program of decision making, either in a church board meeting or in the home of a person in trouble. The following are some basic principles for the selection and training of leaders.

1. *In the development of a pastoral care program, leaders must be selected by the pastor in consultation with people who know that warmth, honesty, and insight are important.* At times, some eager and impulsive people have to be "redirected" when a pastoral program is being formed. A pastor reported that the youth court counseling program in his church would have been jeopardized by volunteers who stressed "speaking in tongues." In his church, the "charismatics" showed little insight into themselves or others. They could have been easily manipulated by offenders with sociopathic tendencies. The warmth of the volunteer would have been misused.

2. *Motivation for program participation should be freely expressed and tested against the needs of*

those who are to be served. This may be accomplished by: *(a)* letting leaders "rise to the surface," as in the group discussions of Wesley Methodist; *(b)* observation of rapport between helper and client, as in the Soteria House program, where untrained youth worked alongside experienced staff members with the mentally ill; *(c)* role playing, verbatim discussions, and analysis of data from client contacts. The training session can combine insights concerning the needs of troubled people with awareness of who we are and how we relate to people.

This philosophy and method can combine emphases that used to be separated: evangelism and pastoral care. The evangelistic emphasis of the group training program at First Baptist Church in Norcross, Georgia, is obvious, yet it leads church members to care for each other and for many persons in a growing community. There is concern without condemnation.

3. *The development of the training program is a demonstration of the warmth, insight, and honesty that is required of gracious counselors.* Planning for the program encourages expression of personal goals and evaluation of stated purposes of the organization. The pastor, or organizer, asks: "What are our reasons for attempting this work?" "Why does the church expect this of us?" "What reasons

can we give for our commitment to this ministry?"

The stated goals are broad enough for experimentation, mistakes, personal ways of doing things. We set limits, establish objectives, but also stress creativity and initiative.

Organizational or program objectives are measured against the preferences and abilities of the training group. When people describe what they think they can and cannot do, they are practicing the honesty that is an essential part of good pastoral care. At the same time, the structuring of a learning situation will encourage members to express warm encouragement to each other and make comments that develop insight and understanding of others. The characteristics of successful care are used to train those who care.

The design of the learning experience will reflect the stated needs of the trainees for help in areas where they are not proficient care-givers. The areas of need can usually be written on a blackboard in one of the first sessions. Some of the statements will be very specific: "How do I start talking to someone about his or her trouble?" "How do I find my way to the patient's room in a mental hospital?" "Will the jailor let me in—and out?" Others are more general: "Will people accept us as pastors?" "Will they think we are nosy?" "How can I talk to a person about trouble that I haven't experienced myself?"

The pastor and several members may classify these questions and return to the next meeting with a structure to meet the expressed needs. The organization may follow some of the content modeled in the previous chapter, or be directed toward one general area of concern. For example, the Clinton, Mississippi, program began with the sponsorship of juvenile offenders.

This method teaches the church officers and others a way of problem solving for many individual needs. As the members begin visitation, they may find a former mental patient who seems to be in good contact with reality but has low self-esteem and poor job skills. When the visitors have helped him to state the areas in which he needs competence, they have followed the same procedure as in their own training.

The resources of learning will come primarily from the learners themselves. This is a basic principle of adult education. Grown people usually know enough about life to supply examples and insights into most of the areas of human need they will contact as pastors. Questions like "Who has seen something like this case before?" "How has this problem been handled in your experience with people?" will draw this experience out of the group. (Chapter 5 will present more ways of relating to experience.)

More technical or institutional problems are discussed by the resource persons who visit the group from a social agency, college, or hospital. They provide a perspective and explain procedures.

But the "authorities" do not determine how the church officers will relate to people in trouble. The interaction of an expert with individual members of the training group will tell the pastor much about a member's attitude toward authority. A continual barrage of "Doctor, don't you think . . ." is a sign that someone is very dependent, or anxious to get additional strength for a doubtful position. The more equality of expression, as authority and members look at a problem together, the better chances there are for a leavening influence of the church in the community.

Evaluation of the learning experiences is to be shared by the group. This is where the "fruit of the spirit" appears, or disappears. Some members can graciously show the mistakes of another and accept criticisms of their own interviews. Others project blame, divert the group from its performance, make excuses, or act as though they don't really care.

This part of training may cause uneasiness in those who have heard of marathon therapy sessions in which people take each other apart. A pastor who allows that kind of analysis in a training program is confusing the therapy of neurotics with the training of healthy leaders. A more realistic approach has been developed in the Duke Street Church, which focuses the training of deacons upon relations with people in distress and shared opinions about these interactions. "Relationship agenda" items—family, job, and other personal matters—in a deacon's life are to be discussed privately with the pastor or in a "personal growth group."

The evaluation is to be specifically related to the theological objectives of pastoral care. We may ask: "Does this attitude toward a person demonstrate the kind of concern that we associate with the life of Christ, or do we find some other possible readings of this relationship?" "Just what are people seeing in us?"

What about the church's acceptance of our statements that Christ cares for the delinquent, the alcoholic, the divorcee? We must evaluate doing as well as feeling. Can we fulfill our promises and keep our programs going?

4. *The pastor serves as a player-coach in the training sessions and exercises.* A comprehensive pastoral care program is an extension of the pastor's attitudes and activities through church leaders to a wider and deeper fellowship. Pastoral consideration for church leaders and concern for those in trouble are role models and spiritual indicators of ministry.

CHAPTER FIVE

Training in Church-Community Systems

The coaching of those who care must begin with our first question of participant management: "What is the mission of this church?" When motivation for ministry has been clarified, a specific program of training can develop.

Motivation for Ministry

The specific theological objectives of lay people may vary from "affirming the essential humanity of God's people" to personal evangelism and a drive for church membership. Within that spectrum, there are at least four themes that appear in correspondence and descriptions of programs.

First, there is the theme of *personal commitment* which combines proclamation with dedication. In biblical terms, we are to "teach and urge" the elders in their duties (1 Timothy 6:2). The witness to truth is to be combined with an expectation of commitment in response. This would be the spirit in which a pastor would structure a training program for the care of people. Facts would be learned, but in a situation where persons could show how they feel about others.

This sense of personal involvement, the combination of knowledge and dedication, is the first objective of a pastoral training program. Hope, expectancy, and urgency are blended with instruction, analysis, and evaluation.

Commitment is a prerequisite, or at least an ingredient of a second objective, the practice of the *priesthood of believers.* As several evaluations of training programs have shown, both congregation and leaders believed that they should be more active in care for each other, or anyone in distress.

The problem with some training programs is an inability to develop a model of ministry for lay people. The older "professional" model is perpetuated when authorities from various fields lecture to deacons or lead seminars in which the laity is warned against "getting involved" or "getting over their heads." Such warnings about the general practice of support and guidance of individuals in trouble are seldom needed. If lay people get into more complex situations, it usually is in an institutional setting where they can work with other staff members to learn how to handle themselves and clients.

The recommendations for training in this chapter

will stress commitment, function, and community action. This may avoid the traditional professional characteristics of aloofness, academic credential barriers, and locus of treatment in an institution.

A third objective is an extension of the second, to build up the *sense of fellowship* in a congregation, to let people experience care and concern. This is "building up the body of Christ." This objective requires that a training program in pastoral care would operate within the church organization, and that an objective of care would be a closer relation of people to a Christian community. In most cases this would be a church, probably the one that has provided the ministry. But there are occasions when a person is more comfortable in a more specialized group. The choice might be on the basis of theology. Robert Ferm found a number of converts from Billy Graham Crusades who found their only fellowship in a Bible study group in a school or in the home of another convert.[1] Or the decision might come from a particular concept of the church. The "house church," which stresses small group fellowship in the homes of adherents, is one means for committed persons to experience closeness in worship and participate in social service.

[1] Robert O. Ferm, *Persuaded to Live* (Old Tappan, N.J.: Fleming H. Revell Company, 1958), pp. 93, 125, 164.

Sometimes the extracongregational group is formed to meet the needs of deprived people. The deprivation may be economic, which prevents a person from traveling some distance to a church building or appearing in presentable clothes, or it may be psychological, which causes discomfort in the presence of "straight," socially successful people. Under such circumstances the church goes to those who need a different form of fellowship. It may be a fellowship house, as in Houston, Texas, where members of Episcopal and other churches live in downtown rooming houses large enough to accommodate alcoholics, parolees for adult offenses, or any persons who need a friend and fellowship.

This extension of an organization out into the community through smaller groups may lead to less building of new sanctuaries and educational space and more supplies for services through house churches' fellowship and halfway houses. In describing the lay renewal and small group ministries of the First Baptist Church in Norcross, Georgia, Pastor Lewis Abbott predicted most of the evangelistic growth through Bible study, worship, and problem-solving groups in homes or buildings outside the church. This would be followed by a stable organization of these groups in various parts of the town. The parent organization and church building would serve as a resource center and a place for specialized ministries.

If the church develops a fellowship that extends into the community, it can meet a fourth characteristic of pastoral care, the *"leaven in the loaf"* parable of the kingdom of God. The leavening influence may be seen in the Christian's quality of life, whatever his or her organizational identification may be. This influence has usually been associated with the personal qualities presented by the apostle Paul in the fifth chapter of Galatians: "love, joy, peace, patience, kindness, goodness, faithfulness, gentleness, self-control." These are necessary moral ingredients of any helping relationship. They are similar to the characteristics of successful therapists that had been identified in the research of Charles B. Truax and others: understanding, warmth, and genuineness.[2] They apply across the boundaries of various theories of therapy. It is the personality that counts, not the school of thought.

This finding offers freedom to lay people who are willing to work with professionals in a variety of community agencies or projects. The contribution of the volunteer is not to be evaluated in terms of

[2]Charles B. Truax, "Effective Ingredients in Psychotherapy," *Journal of Counseling Psychology,* vol. 10, no. 3 (Fall, 1963), pp. 256-263.

academic degrees or membership in professional societies, but by the quality of relationships that he or she develops under the general supervision of a staff member.

In like manner, the lay person can feel confident that the contribution to the life of another in distress does not depend upon the academic training of a minister or adherence to specific theological doctrines. The love of Christ is not bound by a creed or dependent upon academic degrees.

Furthermore, the "leaven" of lay people may be active in a variety of settings. The kingdom of God is not confined to a church building or program, nor is it contaminated by associations with private or public organizations. Our service for Christ may be as real in a social-service agency as it would in a church visitation program.

The Systems Concept

These assumptions, closely related to Jesus' parables of the kingdom of God, sound like the modern theories of "systems analysis" in organizations. That is, people live in a variety of situations: family, work, church, social group, county government. Each organization has an influence upon the individual and upon each other. To be realistic, an organization, such as a church, must recognize its place alongside of other organizations in society and concentrate upon the distinctive emphasis it makes throughout the community. Church members are continually influencing and being influenced by many programs.

The church does not shield its members from these associations but does prepare them for life in the world through a process of moral dialogue. We talk about what is most important, where we find strength, what are our weaknesses, and why we go on living. This is a process that crosses boundaries of clergy-laity, church-community. It sets some comprehensive goals for pastoral care that move beyond the more restrictive emphases of the 1940–1960 era of specialization and professional categories of service:

Systems concept	Specialization
Open dedication to a mission	Personal reservation before nonprofessionals
Utilization of persons according to their talents	Levels of treatment related to academic degrees and accreditation
Relation of clients to a group of concerned people	Relation of the client to the individual therapist
Interrelationships of helping organizations	Institutions claimed for control by specific professions

Relating to Systems

After we have established the basic concepts for a pastoral care program, we are ready to ask: "How do we enter the social systems of the community?"

Just what are these "systems"? The Urban Training Center in Chicago and the Urban Ministry Program at Western Reserve University defined five "gross categories for the major processes of our society":

1. *Socialization systems:* family, school, church, and neighborhood serve the developmental needs of an individual.

2. *Economic productive systems:* businesses, industries, and professional groups produce goods and services necessary for physical and social needs of the individual, and provide work opportunities.

3. *Special care systems:* public housing, anti-poverty, welfare organizations, hospitals, and correctional institutions meet the needs of individuals in trouble.

4. *Central governmental and legal systems:* levels of government, political parties meet the needs for justice and order in society.

5. *Culturally creative systems:* higher education, the arts, and mass media create and disseminate the symbols and theories which express our purpose in

living together in communities and in society.[3]

How do pastors and congregations relate to the other systems in their community? In an interdenominational survey, J. Alan Winter and Edgar W. Mills found few contacts of pastors with government officials or important private citizens if the congregation had no direct or supportive contact with a community agency. But if the congregation is dealing with contemporary issues, the pastor has many secular contacts concerning social problems.

The researchers noted that the time taken for community contacts went up as time spent in church administration went down, and vice versa. Time spent on sermon preparation and pastoral care was not affected.[4]

I mention this finding first to dramatize the importance of congregational attitudes toward the community. The pastor should look within the leadership of the church for help in deciding how to enter the other social systems. Usually there will be

[3] See Robert H. Bonthius, "Pastoral Care for Structures—As Well as Persons," *Pastoral Psychology,* vol. 18, no. 174 (May, 1967), p. 17.

[4] J. Alan Winter and Edgar W. Mills, "Relationships Among the Activities and Attitudes of Christian Clergymen: A Preliminary Report" (Washington, D.C.: Ministry Studies Board, 1968), pp. 6, 12.

men and women who are active in any of the systems to which the church might relate: chamber of commerce, labor unions, League of Women Voters, welfare and hospital boards. If these people are not readily identified, they may respond to comments in sermons.

Lay people will often volunteer to introduce their pastor to community programs in which they have a part. If they do not ask, the pastor can. In the company of a church member, a pastor can meet specific organizations and can obtain a general view of the world in which the people live. The more general perspective can often come from a fire inspector, city manager, or police chief.

A church planning council or official board may with the pastor list the people or organizations to which he or she should be introduced. When this is done, the idea of visitation may broaden. The session of an Atlanta suburban church, Trinity Presbyterian, chartered a bus and took two days for on-the-spot conferences with government officials, welfare workers, and others who met the daily problems of people in whom the church should be interested.

In a smaller community, relating to systems is a function of walking and talking. The pastor of a Virginia coal-mining village church estimated that 90 percent of his members and prospects lived within five hundred yards of the church. If he walked down the main street on Saturday afternoon, he met most of them.

The talking will usually center in a drugstore where mayor, city councilmen, ministers, and businessmen meet for morning coffee.

Pastoral Functions in the Community

The purpose of systems entry is more than recruiting for church membership or showing off the new minister. It should inaugurate: (1) connections between church and specific agencies; (2) channels for formal and informal communication; (3) opportunities for consultation; (4) and development of pastoral and other care programs.

An example of the *connecting* function is the Court House Chaplaincy in Newton, Kansas. Theological students and community clergy developed a regular visitation program to people before the time of hearings or in the jail. In time, they also became the counselors of courthouse employees.

Negotiations with county officials began with the ministerial alliance. Supervision of clergy came from a chaplain at Prairie View Mental Health Center. In time, the sheriff and others began to trust the students and pastors, especially after a logbook was opened in the jail so that clergy could sign in and out, specify their clients, and summarize the content of their visits.[5]

The *communicating* function may be informal or may take the form of joint decision by clergy and other professionals in an agency or church setting. In a neighborhood church clinic, Church of the Good Shepherd, a volunteer met every client at the door and introduced him or her to one of the pastors or seminarians on duty. The clergyperson discussed any stress areas in the client's life. The volunteer then introduced the client to others who were waiting to see the physician of the clinic. Pastor and physician saw the client together and discussed the need for joint or separate follow-up. The pastor followed the client through a home visit.

A physician who was asked about the clinic described a "real health care" example. He had treated a boy for a spider bite. The boy returned later with another bite and was taken to the clinic. After treatment, the pastor on duty went with the boy to his apartment and found the spider webs in the basement. He persuaded the landlord to clean out the area and spray for insects.[6]

[5] Robert Carlson, "The Court-House Chaplaincy—A Project in Collaboration," *Pastoral Psychology,* vol. 23, no. 231 (September, 1972), pp. 18-26.
[6] Granger Westberg, "Contextual Teaching of Pastoral Care in a Neighborhood Church Clinic," in *Explorations in Ministry,* ed. G. Douglass Lewis (New York: IDOC, 1971), pp. 176-185.

Consultation usually evolves from the establishment of regular communication. In Vance County, North Carolina, half of the ministers in a rural area attended seminars over a three-year period to develop relationship-building skills and to work with a consultant from the mental health center on general topics in pastoral care. As a result, the clergy carried more difficult cases without discomfort because they had the backup of specialists, and referrals from clergy to the mental health center were more productive because of the relationships established.[7]

The consultations were more productive because mental health professionals had learned the functions of pastors in the community, and the clergy had discovered who they were and what they could do. That is, the pastors knew what they wanted. If they needed some reassurance or advice about a parishioner whom they were counseling, they would ask for "consultation." On the other hand, if they saw that the problem was beyond their training, or a relationship was blocked, they would propose "referral." These terms are in quotation marks to emphasize their distinctiveness. Untrained clergy may confuse them and try to make a referral when

[7]"Creating Alternatives to Clinical Care," (Chapel Hill, N.C.: Division of Community Psychiatry, 1973), p 13

the persons only need consultation, or vice versa.[8]

Care and counseling are appropriately shared by church and community when this function is preceded by connecting, communicating, and consulting. These functions are also basic to the training course for lay people who will share with the pastor in a preventative, crisis, or maintenance ministry.

The Spirit and Content of Training

Lay people who function as pastors prefer practice under supervision rather than hour-long lectures. They are adults with experience that not only adds to the specifics of a lecture, but also gives them confidence to try out what they are learning. A "mini-lecture" may be necessary to introduce a topic or summarize a discussion, but adults are usually ready to make their own contribution if we give them a chance. After all, they live every day in the systems that are basic to our care of individuals. They know what people are facing and have some success in coping with life in the world.

The following content is built around topics familiar to lay people. One caution should be raised. Do not be satisfied with the topics

[8]See James B. Ashbrook, *Responding to Human Pain* (Valley Forge: Judson Press, 1975), chapter 10 for a discussion of the referral process.

themselves, which are essentially functional and secular rather than theological. Use each topic as an opportunity to ask how belief and Christian practice are resources. Encourage lay people to say how they would relate faith to a specific situation, and ask what they would pray for and with whom. Again and again, lay people say that supervised ministry gives them a new perspective on the church and a deeper appreciation of their faith. Create opportunities for them to tell others how this is so.

A training program to meet the objectives of systematic pastoral care would include the following categories of information.

Human Development and Response to Stress

Pastoral care is for the adequate as well as the inadequate. Much of the conversation in a weekly group meeting, or in visitation by a deacon, would be classified as "edifying" rather than remedial or crisis-oriented. The great advantage of systematic pastoral care over a clergy-oriented system is the opportunity to cultivate people before a crisis, to assist people in moral decision making while they still have adequate social standing and emotional stability.

A comprehensive program will stress normal growth and development rather than pathology-oriented sequences like "oral, anal, phallic." For the

Christian, the developmental scheme should be oriented toward theological and moral categories, as Lewis Sherrill wrote in *The Struggle of the Soul.* He discusses the religious, emotional, and social implications of each stage of life:

Childhood: becoming an individual

Adolescence: becoming weaned away from parents

Young maturity: finding one's basic identifications

Middle life: achieving a mature view of life and the universe

Old age: simplification of life.[9]

In a discussion of these stages, a training group will need to consider some cases to distinguish adequate from inadequate adjustment. Usually a group of mature adults can furnish its own case studies. This increases the relevance of the training and also increases personal insight, for an individual often sees himself or herself in the neighbor or family member that is presented for review by others.

Along with a discussion of developmental stages there should be some attention to the situational factors that support or inhibit personal develop-

[9]Lewis J. Sherrill, *The Struggle of the Soul* (New York: The Macmillan Company, 1962), p. 9.

ment. Charles Kemp's *Pastoral Care with the Poor* will open the eyes of some church leaders to the conditions that twist and thwart the normal growth of persons.[10]

The typical reactions to stress in life have been outlined by Anton Boisen in *Religion in Crisis and Custom.*[11] One reaction is drifting, a condition of apathy, lack of initiative, helplessness. When this condition is encountered, church leaders often need the insights of someone who has been in the same condition as those who are drifting. This person can tell what motivates or discourages those who seem to accept anything that happens.

A second reaction is concealment. This is usually manifest in cynicism, faultfinding, intolerance, excessive meticulousness, restlessness, self-importance, bitterness, continuous anxiety, and self-pity. Any difficulties are blamed upon others or upon personal illness. An elaborate scheme of defense is erected against personal responsibilities.

A third reaction is confrontation. In *Light Beyond Shadows,* a pastor, Frederick West, writes of his decision in a mental hospital to admit openly to himself and others some of the failures of his life

[10]Charles F. Kemp, *Pastoral Care with the Poor* (Nashville: Abingdon Press, 1972).

[11]Anton T. Boisen, *Religion in Crisis and Custom* (New York: Harper & Row, Publishers, 1955), pp. 41-53.

without excuse.[12] This was the turning point for him. There were later difficulties, as with parishioners who were uneasy in the presence of an honest clergyman, but he was a healthier man with the three-fourths of the congregation that stayed with him. And he felt that the congregation was healthier, too.

As Mr. West could testify, a frank awareness of limitations does not mean that a person is completely responsible for everything that happens to one or around one. Awareness without defensiveness means that we know more of what we can do and what we must depend on others to do.

When these reactions to stress are presented, men and women can give their own examples of concealment and confrontation. If members are being trained as group leaders, they can discuss the ways in which they or others in a group manifest any of these reactions. The leaders for groups in the Duke Street Church met regularly with the pastor to identify and interpret these and other types of behavior.

If members are being trained as pastors for a section of the membership, the interviews that they write up after a visit can often supply direct evidence

[12]Frederick West, *Light Beyond Shadows* (New York: The Macmillan Company, 1960).

of any of the three reactions to stress—including those of the lay pastor.

Family and Community Relationships

A comprehensive program of care will consider the individual in the family and in the community. This requires training in three aspects of the social forces that support or hurt a person:

1. The *power structure.* Who is a leader to the individual in trouble, or what loss of leadership has caused him or her trouble? This question helps us explain why people who have been "getting along" for years will become anxious, depressed, impulsive, or disoriented when the dominant member of a family dies, loses a job, or becomes ill. Widows look for a new leader in son or daughter, brother, pastor, banker, or lawyer.

Ask the training seminar to name some leaders of the church or community in the past, the relationships of people to them, and the adjustments that were necessary when they moved, retired, or died.

2. The *individual's assignment* in the structure of family and society. Role conflicts are common determinants of unhappiness and anxiety. A son or daughter may not wish to take a father's place in decision making for a widow. A divorcee is burdened by the twin responsibilities of motherly

acceptance and firm discipline of small children. A father is depressed because of a demotion or dismissal that reduces his ability to provide for his family and to feel significant with his colleagues.

Consider with your group an example of someone in trouble and ask: "What caused this person to feel insignificant?" "What has changed?" "What would restore significance?"

An important part of this assignment of role in family or community is the way in which significance is *communicated.* What did the wife say to the husband when he was demoted or dismissed? "Role play" a scene in which a wife is accepting and one in which a wife is threatened by this perceived loss of status.

3. The *balance of leadership and role* in family and community. Like the body, the family, church, and society are made up of diverse elements which can conflict if there is no balancing of drives toward some common objectives. Mutual recognition in a family brings balance. On the other hand, favoritism and ascription of failure to another member will bring sibling rivalry, withdrawal of the father, or overbearing responsibility to the mother.

Describe the problems of a daughter who is always expected to succeed so that the mother will feel socially significant and the father feel reassured as a successful human being. Try to diagram some of the ways in which these people are relating.

Who can give examples of the same process of balancing in the larger, extended family, or at work, or in the church? What happens when the daughter leaves home, or a son rebels, or a "balancing" manager is promoted and the next boss plays favorites?

When a group begins to talk about these three forces for family and community stability, the examples may seem so ordinary that we do not see how decisive a disturbance of daily structure is for personal well-being. But in a mental health crisis center, 80 percent of the patients reported a real or threatened separation in their social structure as the main reason for their difficulties. In some ways they were psychologically displaced, put down, or shoved out.[13]

Church and Community Services

A balanced system of care will combine a knowledge of personal development and character with an awareness of the ways in which home and culture develop or detract from individual growth and stability.

[13] Paul Polak, "Social Systems Intervention," *Archives of General Psychiatry,* vol. 25, no. 2 (August, 1971), pp. 111-113.

This is possible when church and community cooperate in the care of individuals of families. The church will take the lead in character building and emphasize strong family support for children. A community agency would provide specialized psychiatric services for severely disturbed children. At times there would be a combination in which a county budget would pay for the workers in a kindergarten for mentally retarded children in the educational building of a church.

A training seminar should stress these connections through a discussion of services under general categories of help rather than types of agencies (religious, county, private, general, or mental hospital). The emphasis would be upon the function needed to meet demands. Any one function might be met by several agencies (for example, "personality development" is a concern of church, private counselor), or one agency might fulfill several functions.

What are the major functional categories of systematic pastoral care?

1. *Immediate service.* This includes crisis calls, such as in the case of death or emergency. Guidance for the training group may come from the pastor, emergency-room personnel, or county rescue squad.

Another part of immediate service is screening

("What kind of help do you need?") and disposition ("Where can you get the kind of help you need?"). The intake worker at a local mental health center or a county nurse in the health department would be a helpful teacher of church leaders concerning these questions.

The questions need special stress with church workers because people often call for a pastor when they have some generalized anxiety and are not really sure of the source of their difficulties.

Another question under immediate services is classification. What is the relation of this person to Christ, the church, the community? What is his or her direction of growth or disintegration? These questions can be grouped under the categories discussed in chapter 2: prospects, the growing, the faithful, the careless, the distressed, the isolated.

A monthly compilation of estimates in each category will assist the pastor and church leaders in the establishment of programs to meet specific needs. For example, is the percentage of "distressed" above 50 percent of all visits? What types of distress exist? The First Baptist Church in Norcross, Georgia, found so many young adult divorcees during lay renewal visitations that a specific program was developed for these adults. The pastor reported that when one of the group remarried, all the others attended the wedding, along with other well-wishers from the church. One recent visitor to the group, who had been rejected by another church because of her divorce and theological questions, was so moved by this expression of fellowship that she said to a companion, "I'll go to Sunday school with you. This church has something for me."

2. *Stabilization of health or behavior.* This is most often a community responsibility, in a general hospital, city jail, or mental health center. A physician, nurse, jailer, or psychologist may tell how a physical or emotional condition may "flare up" and be controlled.

Some churches and hospitals give special attention to the training of lay people for this category of care. The Christ Hospital in Cincinnati, Ohio, provides biweekly case seminars and didactic presentations for volunteer assistants to the chaplains. For four months, the volunteers write verbatim interviews for seminar discussion. Readings in the field of pastoral care are also required. Persons chosen to continue as volunteers are responsible for leadership of one seminar a year. They attend the biweekly seminars and have an individual conference with a chaplain at least once every four months.

3. *Social and spiritual maintenance.* As Charles Glock noted in his study of Episcopal lay people,

comfort rather than challenge is expected from the church by widows, widowers, or any persons who are financially or socially disadvantaged.[14] The visitation of shut-ins has been one of the most common activities promoted through church-visitor programs.

In addition to visitation programs, churches have developed groups for senior citizens, the newly married, first parents, divorced, or parents with an "empty nest" (when the last child has left for college). These groups are the first line of defense and the first to be called in any crisis by a member. When a baby in the "first parents" group died, the other four couples in their fellowship were the first to come and the last to leave their friends.

Sometimes the church, like the social agency, has organized a "halfway house" for support of the socially or psychologically disadvantaged. Usually this is a rented house in the rooming-house or transient area of a city where a couple from the church or a Salvation Army officer arranges lodging, coordinates preparation of meals, counsels individuals, and oversees group discussions. If the clients stay more than a few weeks, some become monitors for various tasks to be performed.

[14]Charles Y. Glock, Benjamin B. Ringer, and Earl R. Babbie, *To Comfort and To Challenge* (Berkeley: University of California Press, 1967), p. 205.

Those who are met "halfway" are youthful runaways, drug abusers, chronic alcoholics, patients released from a mental hospital, families evicted from their homes, and adult offender parolees.

Clients are encouraged to take as much responsibility as possible for meals, cleaning, crises with other residents, jobs, and bills. The programs are designed to increase interdependence and to reduce dependence.

Some persons need this transitional living facility once or twice as they recover self-esteem after some overwhelming failure or loss. Others need more than support. They are so socially inept or occupationally unskilled that specific training is necessary.

Social and spiritual support may need to be extended from the church into other institutions, such as jails or prisons. In New Mexico, church lay people visit a prisoner who is scheduled for parole in one year. During that year, they discuss life on the outside, "how to make it," and what is happening in the family, if the inmate has one. As parole approaches, the two may leave the prison together for a ball game in a nearby city or a visit to the inmate's or layperson's family.

4. *Competence training.* One of the key strengths of the prison visitation program is introduction of

an inmate to a job on the outside. Since the work record of prisoners is often poor before incarceration, and worse upon release, much weight is attached by the prison and parole staff to a steady job. Lay people function in two ways to assist the staff: to increase the parolee's self-respect and impulse control and to sponsor or introduce the parolee to an employer.

Men and women in church leadership positions may not realize the social handicaps of many of the people who contact social agencies or correctional institutions. Some churchwomen in Atlanta, Georgia, discovered that many of the returning patients from a state mental hospital could not plan a meal, keep an orderly house, or look ahead for the needs of children. To remedy this, the women cooperated with concerned church people to develop classes in homemaking, child care, newspaper reading and current events, shopping, and recreation. These were held in a renovated apartment with the name "Community Friendship." Along with these social skills, vocational programs in typing, bookkeeping, cooking, and other semi-skilled tasks were provided by the state office of vocational rehabilitation.

A minority of visitors to a "friendship" house are so emotionally or intellectually handicapped that they cannot obtain competitive employment. They may live at home, or in a rooming house, and spend the day in a "sheltered workshop." They work on contract from local firms to produce work at their own pace. Several church people who were active in the "Community Friendship" program obtained contracts from local banks for envelope stuffing. This could be done by some of the retarded clients with a minimum of supervision.

Competence training, social support, and routine visitation are often part of our ministry to families with some specific difficulty, such as mental retardation. The retarded person often is hidden from the church until systematic visitation makes him or her known to visitors. Since only one-tenth of the mentally retarded are in institutions, lay people soon learn to ask how the children at home, or the adults who wander about the house, may be helped. Then it is time to plan some comprehensive program in the church and community. A special class for the retarded will need to be funded by the school board—which usually contains church people. Businesses, such as cafeterias, must be cultivated to accept trainees for supervised placement and then employment. Churches must agree on a strategic location for a Sunday school center for the retarded, with classes graded by age and sometimes by capability. Then there is the need to cultivate other church people to receive the parents of the retarded into their full fellowship. This may be the most difficult job of all.

The participation of many dedicated people in a training program for pastoral care will be the nucleus of strength for a change in church and community attitudes toward the people who have failed in some conspicuous way. In 1972, Pastor James Porch, of Clinton, Mississippi, began a weekly seminar of youth court staff with lay people of his church to sponsor youth offenders. As the church leaders became more aware of the family conflicts that contributed to the difficulties of the young people with whom they were working, the program was broadened to include Sunday afternoon meetings of many people from the church to discuss parent-child relationships. The gulf between offender and church member was bridged in discussion of common problems in the family.

The church emphasis should be upon coordination and deepening of efforts to assist people in trouble. This can occur in the church through changing attitudes toward acceptance and through continuing training of church leaders as ministers. These lay people can be influential upon community agencies in the allocation of public monies for programs that develop a disadvantaged person's ability to live in the community and adjust to society.

This dual effort is one reason for the cooperation of state and county agency professionals in the training of church people. They realize that there will not only be benefits to the individuals whom they serve, but also wider political support for the maintenance of their programs.

5. *Personal character building.* An increasing number of pastors have received some training in personal counseling. Troubled people request one or more private sessions for the reduction of anxiety, insight into reasons for jealousy or crippling inhibitions, self-control over impulsive actions, or runaway fears. Although some persons report definite benefits, the percentage of those improved through therapy is not much higher than the percentage of equally troubled people who report improvement without therapy.[15]

The most sensible conclusion is that some counselors who are very warm, understanding, and honest are helpful to some persons with particular types of difficulties.[16] If a church develops groups similar to those described by Pastor Owen in Wesley

[15]See chapter 7, "The Evaluation of Therapeutic Outcomes," in *Handbook of Psychotherapy and Behavior Change,* ed. Allen E. Bergin and Sol. L. Garfield (New York: John Wiley & Sons, Inc., 1971).

[16]H. H. Strupp, "Is the Time Right for Comparisons of Therapeutic Techniques?" *Psychotherapy and Social Science Review,* vol. 6, no. 9 (1972), pp. 17-22.

Methodist, the pastor and church leaders will soon know who, over a period of time, is helpful to people with particular personality quirks or situational crises. This characteristic may also be recognized as deacons or others read their verbatim interviews from routine visits or emergency calls.

CHAPTER SIX

Strength from
the Brethren

The first command from Jesus to Simon Peter was "strengthen your brethren" (Luke 22:32). The circle of disciples must be sustained, both by the memory of the Lord's sacrifice and by active concern for each other. In the most dangerous day of his earthly life, Jesus considered the human needs of his leaders.

Could we openly admit our need for someone like Peter to strengthen us? Jesus did. Just before this command, he showed his appreciation for the disciples' fellowship: "You are those who have continued with me in my trials" (Luke 22:28). A few hours later he longed for them to watch with him in the agony of his final decision. Are we as willing as he to ask people for support?

The answer to that question seems to indicate that our practice is a contradiction of our Lord's example. Edgar Mills and John Koval, in a study of twenty-one denominations, found that ministers who relied the most upon prayer, Scripture reading, and trust in God during stress were most likely to report no other help received.[1]

How shall we evaluate this finding? First, it is obvious that a disciple should be like the Lord in looking to the heavenly Father for absolute support. He is our lasting source of strength. The research of Dr. Mills found that prayer and Bible reading did reduce a minister's sense of loneliness. (It also showed that these same ministers were using many informal sources of support, such as the family.)

But, second, the ministers who look only to God in times of personal stress are less satisfied than ministers who seek the support of other professional people. The most satisfactory solution is still found in the example of Jesus, who prayed alone in the garden, but also told his disciples of the anguish of his decisions and sought their companionship. He opened his heart to his friends and to his Father in heaven (John 15:14-15). They were to care for each other as he cared for them.

Third, although ministers are not seeking and receiving the continual fellowship that Jesus sought from his disciples, almost half get some help from superiors or colleagues when the going is tough, as

---

[1]Edgar W. Mills and John P. Koval, *Stress in the Ministry* (Washington, D.C.: Ministry Studies Board, 1971), p. 31.

when they are unemployed, uncertain about their vocation, or admittedly inadequate to handle problems with superiors or pressing demands of the ministry.

From the Mills/Koval research we can see that some ministers are refreshed and guided by their devotional life and by conversations with other ecclesiastical leaders during periods of career stress.

But where are we to find sustenance during the daily fatigue and frustration that accompany a profession in which we are constantly giving and seldom receiving? Jesus' first concern for the disciples after their arduous missionary journey was "come away . . . and rest a while" (Mark 6:31).

The minister's wife is his main source of personal support. Almost a third of the clergymen in the Mills/Koval sample mentioned the spouse as helpful in stress resulting from overwork, frustration, uncertainty about or adjustment to a new job.[2]

As we would expect, the spouse is less helpful when a minister has a mental health problem or difficulty in marriage. This is the category of help in which "other professionals" become significant.

My concern for pastoral care is with the underutilization of the congregation in problems such as "overwork/too much activity" and "frustra-

[2]*Ibid.*, pp. 33-36.

tion with lack of accomplishment." Fourteen percent or less of clergymen sought support from members of the congregation for the issues which were directly related to their work with the congregation.

Some readers may immediately say, "But I have no one to turn to!" I would reply by pointing to the Mills/Koval finding that clergymen reported help received more often than they asked for it. When support was needed, it came because others saw that the minister could use a little help. Only in one case out of three did the minister ask for some assistance or admit that he had more than he could handle.[3]

The Uniqueness of the Pastorate

Why should a minister turn to anyone for support? Is he or she not expected to obtain divine aid alone? The example of Jesus included prayer *and* sharing, lone hours with God *and* expressions of appreciation for those who would watch with him in times of anguish or eat with him when he was troubled.

But this answer misses another part of the question. Is there something *unique* about the ministry that either increases or decreases the need for *personal* support in his or her work?

[3]*Ibid.,* pp. 36-37.

The pastorate is a uniquely personal profession. God calls a person to represent him, to guide others in their understanding of his commands, to be the actual channel of love from God to men and women. This awesome responsibility is confirmed by the church, which looks to the pastor both for expert knowledge of God and a quality of life that will draw others to God. The personal aspects of ordination are especially strong in American Protestantism, which since the eighteenth century has insisted upon a "converted ministry." Intellectual knowledge of and consent to a creed or confession is not enough. Warmth, grace, and conviction are also required.

In addition to these theological expectations, there are so many functions of a parish minister in which character and personal understanding are the major resources. There is no other major profession in which such heavy demands are made upon a *person*. Quality of life is not only a message preached on Sunday, but it is also a measure of daily ministry.

Because of this unique measure the minister must take more care than any other professional for the way in which he or she answers the challenges of relationships with others, proclamation of values, exercise of power, management of change. Since the minister is a *public* professional, advice and support must come from representatives of a voluntary organization, the church, as well as from professional peers or superiors. A minister is a "consumer-oriented" professional.

Ideally, the minister can develop mutually satisfying exchanges with leaders in the congregation, with other ministers, and with community colleagues in person-helping agencies. All these sources of support are needed for the minister to stand in the center of an organization that is continually giving, comforting, guiding. Ministers must not only obey Jesus' command to strengthen the brethren, but also find some brethren to strengthen them.

Acknowledging the Earthen Vessel

The apostle Paul saw the treasure of the gospel in "earthen vessels" (2 Corinthians 4:7). He acknowledged the myriad strains upon his own life as a minister of the Lord Jesus. The question concerning modern ministers is: Where can they find a safe place to admit their feelings as human beings?

A variety of places for opportunities like Interpreter's House, Lake Junaluska, North Carolina, or the Institute for Advanced Pastoral Studies, Bloomfield Hills, Michigan, are available for personal insight and renewal. The most enduring of these centers have combined awareness of the minister's personality with skill training in the fulfillment of ministry. Growth rather than therapy is expected. Carlyle Marney and Jack Birsdorf are providing theory and methods for deepening spiritual life and relating it to all parts of the church's ministry.

The vocational emphasis of these programs is especially important in a day when ministers and others have been misguided into "confrontation" groups. This misdirection was one of the major barriers to the development of understanding between priests and young deacons in a Maryland-D.C. diocesan program of fellowship and supervision:

> a fair number of each group had had unhappy, and in some cases traumatic, experiences with clinical training, sensitivity groups, or psychiatrically oriented individuals or institutions.[4]

We should admit that some criticisms of these groups come because of the individual rigidities of dissatisfied clients, but we should also recognize the difference between a marathon session for neurotic or maladjusted people and a professional seminar in which a minister seeks to understand himself or herself in relation to parishioners.

[4]Robert Mahon, "An Example of the Use of Professional Development Groups in Support of New Ministers," *Pastoral Psychology,* vol. 22, no. 212 (March, 1971), p. 33.

The balance between professional goals and personal insight can be maintained in local or regional centers of training as well as in the national programs. A regional example is the three-month course for parish clergy at Central State Hospital, Milledgeville, Georgia. Under the leadership of Chaplain James L. Travis, clergy from throughout the state spend three or four days of each week in supervised ministries. Some of the visitation is in units of the hospital: adult psychotic, drug addict, alcoholic, mentally retarded. Some of the visits are in the community as representatives of local churches. Supervisory seminars combine discussions on the care of specific patients or parishioners with awareness of the minister's personality as it affects the relationship between minister and patient.

Seminars of this type complement the pastor's development of supportive relationships with congregational leaders. Both seminars and congregational relationships are necessary. The clergy conferences provide a professional perspective. The meeting of pastor with lay ministers offers specific on-the-spot evaluation and analysis, together with offers of help and encouragement. In a very personal profession, like the ministry, we need some meetings in which we see the forest, and others in which we are looking at the trees.

Keep the Faith

Shared associations with lay ministers will maintain the minister's faith because he or she will see some examples of faith in action. But there are many churches in which this program has been opposed or is considered an impossibility. And even if lay associates are active, there still are calls upon the clergy to set values, make decisions, and maintain the integrity of the program. The pastor is expected as leader of the congregation to exemplify and celebrate the caring purposes of the body of Christ.

The requirement to maintain the value of concern for others in the name of God must be met by a combination of resources, for it is a daily and draining demand. There must be renewal and guidance in worship and prayer, Bible study alone and with colleagues, shared experiences of care in visitation with lay people, and conferences in which the minister experiences the importance of moral decision making as a unique professional skill. Like Timothy, we need inspiration and instruction in the values that are central to our profession lest their integrity be lost in the contradictions of life and the contending schools of knowledge that surround us (1 Timothy 6:20-21).

There are two types of professional associations

that help a minister to keep the faith. First, the clergy is reinforced in its care of difficult and dependent people through seminars organized by mental health centers, general hospitals, and other agencies. The staff share with the clergy in techniques to meet emergencies, attitudes to provide long-term care of deprived people, and theories that explain some difficult cases. The minister feels less defeated and more confident of personal worth in these sessions. Why? Because the hospital staff does not accept the ministerial goal of perfection. It challenges the assumption of radical change and usually calls for more moderate objectives, such as modification of behavior or reduction of anxiety. Ministers often find that they are not really expected by anyone but themselves to work miracles and work them alone. Other professions are becoming more accustomed to sharing responsibility, accepting individual limitations. There are continual warnings in technical meetings about "messianic complexes," grandiose feelings that the power and wisdom of one staff member will cure all the ills of a difficult client.

The other source of support for "value maintenance" is the weekly, monthly, or quarterly meetings of pastors in a geographic region, denominationally or interdenominationally. Traditionally, these assemblies were developed for mutual edification but have turned more toward ecclesiastical business sessions. The Washington Episcopal Clergy Association has sought to reverse this trend through regular meetings to develop "a spirit of brotherhood in the relationships of clergy to replace the poison of competition."[5] After discussing an area of concern, such as professional responsibilities and standards, a committee is requested to bring in a report. When presented as a paper for all the members, there is discussion and refinement of the document. The statement then becomes Association policy.

This type of professional organization maintains high morale because members are discussing the issues that encourage or discourage long term commitment to a profession. Mutual concern, trust, concerted action, and shared wisdom convey the faith of others in us and our ideals so that we can keep the faith with them.

Share the Power

A personal function of the pastor is to increase the commitment of congregational leaders toward desired spiritual goals. The philosophy and techniques for this sharing of power were developed in

[5] Edward R. Sims, "WECA—A Response to Passivity and Isolation Among Parish Ministers," *Pastoral Psychology*, Vol. 22, no. 212 (March, 1971), p. 46.

denominational programs of the late sixties. The process of planning and action used by the United Church of Christ was developed in local churches which asked these questions:

Who are we as a church? (Clarifying Our Identity)
Where are we? (Defining the World's Situation)
What are we doing? (Self-Study)
What new behavior do we propose? (Action)
How are we doing? (Evaluation)
How do we rejoice? (Celebration)[6]

Training in these and similar questions was offered in denominational and council of churches' workshops for pastors and denominational officials. The advantage of this planning process over the usual promotional package from ecclesiastical headquarters was the opportunity for the pastor to mobilize the power of lay people in consensus. The pastor was not pushing or pulling all alone. The pastor was an enabler for others, helping the leadership define organizational purposes, clarify motivation, shape a program, and mobilize resources.

The planning process for churches grew out of a concern for a change in church structure that would lead the congregation toward service and action in

[6]"The Local Church in God's Mission." (United Church of Christ, 1967), p. 13. See also Gerald J. Jud, *Pilgrim's Process* (Philadelphia: United Church Press, 1967).

the world. Thus, the planning process itself has been one source of support to clergy who were ready to "rock the ark."

Comprehensive programs of instruction on change have been developed in urban training centers and in theological seminaries. The Continuing Education Program of Virginia Theological Seminary provides six weeks on personal change, theological change, social change, and institutional change. There is a year of follow-up and continuing education back home in the parish.[7]

Sometimes ministers are specifically concerned about change in themselves or in their occupation. Career Development Centers in major cities have been established to meet this need through three days of intensive assessment and counsel. Since primary support comes from denominational budgets, ministers know that this is their fellowship's effort to assist them personally and vocationally. In many instances, the testing period convinces a minister that he or she could go into another vocation if he or she wanted to. This increases self-esteem, lowers the sense of being trapped in the ministry, and often leads to a reaffirmation of the call to serve God *freely* through

[7]Bennett J. Sims, "Continuing Education as a Peer Support Experience in the Dynamics of Change," *Pastoral Psychology*, vol. 22, no. 212 (March, 1971), p. 41.

a church vocation rather than a redirection.[8]

The process through which a minister arrives at a career decision is similar to that which we have described for the organization of a comprehensive care program or the guidance of a troubled person in decision making. The physician of souls finds personal healing in the same way that he or she would offer help to a parishioner.

In the congregation, the motivation that pushes along the process of change is often a lay renewal movement. As Grace Goodman found in her study of congregations that changed toward more concern for each other and the community, the basic precondition for change was the presence of a group of people with a conviction about the new mission of the church, an openness to hear and follow further insights, and commitment to action. The particular process of renewal was different in every church, but there always was work through small groups and a minister who was willing and able to work *with* the people.

There were two results of mutual care between pastor and people: members were revitalized and

---

[8]Thomas E. Brown, "Career Counseling as a Form of Pastoral Care," *Pastoral Psychology,* vol. 22, no. 212 (March, 1971), p. 19. For a description of the development of these programs, see Fred Petri, "Career Counseling for Professional Church Leaders," *Pastoral Psychology,* vol. 22, no. 211 (February, 1971), pp. 49-55.

the church became a force of witness and service in the community.[9] Programs can be developed through "strengthening the brethren" to care for the whole flock of God.

[9]Grace Ann Goodman, *Rocking the Ark* (New York: Board of National Missions, United Presbyterian Church in the U.S.A., 1968), p. 211.

Appendix

The cassette tape which accompanies *Comprehensive Pastoral Care* in the Judson Tape'n' Text package contains interviews by the author, Samuel Southard, with pastors and counselors who have had experience in working with systematic programs of pastoral care like those described in the book.

SIDE A:

Louis Abbott, Pastor of the First Baptist Church of Norcross, Georgia, discusses how groups can be established in the local church to carry on lay ministries of pastoral care.

Ron Sunderland, Professor at the Institute of Religion, Texas Medical Center, Houston, Texas, suggests ways in which lay persons can be selected and trained for participation in the ministry of pastoral care.

Bill Jackson, Director of the HUB, Center for the Care of Families, Decatur, Georgia, tells how pastors can work with community agencies in making referrals of individuals who need help the pastor is not qualified to give.

SIDE B:

Richard McKay, Chaplain Supervisor of the Wake County Hospital System in Raleigh, North Carolina, describes how support groups for ministers can be established.

Ed Storey, Minister of Ministries and Missions at the New Hope Baptist Church of Raleigh, North Carolina, relates the ministry of lay people in pastoral care to the lay renewal movement which conveys a broader concept of lay ministry.

Richard McKay and Ed Storey discuss the relationship of pastors to the lay renewal movement.